The BELGIAN COOKBOOK

ENID GORDON
MIDGE SHIRLEY

Drawings by Charles Burton

MACDONALD & CO
LONDON & SYDNEY

A MACDONALD BOOK
© Text: Enid Gordon and Midge Shirley, 1982 © Drawings: Charles Burton, 1982
Designed by Enid Gordon

First published in Great Britain in 1983 by Macdonald & Co (Publishers) Ltd, London & Sydney

 A member of BPCC plc

ISBN 0 356 09501 0

Macdonald & Co (Publishers) Ltd
Maxwell House
74 Worship Street
London EC2A 2EN

Phototypeset by Jean-Marie Dessambre, Thon.
Text and illustrations printed in Belgium by Offset-Printing Van Den Bossche n.v., Mechelen.

Sources of illustrations
The photographs on the following pages are reproduced by kind permission of the Musée de la
Vie Wallonne, Liège: 2-3, 25, 30, 31, 51, 64, 120-1, 130, 136-7, 143, 144, 152, 158(a), 158(b), 168-9,
170, 178, 196(a), 196(b), 199, 210.

All other photographs come from private collections.

Illustration pages 2-3
Harvesters' Lunch, 1912.

acknowledgements

We should like to thank, first and foremost, all the members of the Tuesday Group for their energy and enthusiasm in getting this book published ; Connie Sepulchre, who first suggested the idea of a book on Belgian cooking ; Charles Burton, who produced a wealth of wonderful drawings ; and André Kirchberger and Barney Trench for their unfailingly cheerful support and practical help.

We should also like to thank Messieurs Jean Fraikin and Yves Moreau of the Musée de la Vie Wallonne, in Liège, for their permission to reproduce a number of the superb photographs in the Museum's collection, and Madame Hélène Poelemans and Monsieur Jacques Vander Syp of Offset-Printing Van den Bossche for their kind help and expertise.

Last but far from least, to all the individuals and institutions who gave us their material, practical and moral support, our warmest thanks. Without them this book would never have seen the light of day.

contents

Market day at Veurne

introduction

Anybody who has been to Belgium will tell you that it is one of the few countries in the world where the food served in restaurants and private houses is consistently good. But ask the same people about regional Belgian cooking and more often than not you will draw a blank. Many will mumble about waterzooi, carbonnades or eels in green sauce but how many of these will have heard of *oie à l'instar de Visé, tarte a l'djotte*, or any of the hundreds of specialities that are the patrimony of a country in which folklore and traditional cooking are still part of everyday life ?

The reputation of Belgian cuisine suffered greatly in the past from the proximity of France and an occasional similarity with French dishes in the cooking of some of the Walloon provinces and Western Flanders. Comparison with such a formidable neighbour was daunting, to say the least, especially in the nineteenth century, when French taste and dogmatism in culinary matters reigned supreme. Nor did certain historical events help. The settling in Belgium, for instance, of a large, over-critical and vociferous group of French political exiles, after Napoleon III's coup d'état in 1852, was instrumental in helping to promote the image of culinary underdevelopment in Belgian cuisine, an image which Francophile Belgian gastronomes did nothing to discourage and that prevailed until recent years, when a growing sense of regional identity and a renewal of interest in « authentic » cooking led to a reappraisal of the cuisine of the Belgian provinces.

What indeed could be further removed from Baudelaire's reiterated and unfounded complaints about Belgian food in *Pauvre Belgique* than the great gastronome Curnonsky's statement that « with French cooking, Belgian cuisine is the best in the world ».

Whether they are Flemish or Walloon, whether they like substantial country dishes or the comforting delights of *cuisine ménagère*, whether or not they have the discriminating palate of an epicure, all Belgians love to eat. Together with the quality of the cooking, something that never fails to strike visitors to Belgium is the quantity of food absorbed and the size of portions in restaurants. This is not new. When Victor Hugo was a political exile in Brussels, a man sitting at the next table in a restaurant said to him : « You must surely be French to eat such a vast quantity of bread ». Hugo replied in his usual gruff manner : « And you must surely be Belgian to eat such a vast quantity of everything ! »

The Belgians are and have always been the *bons vivants* of Europe — just look at the rabelaisian scenes that run through Flemish painting, from Breughel to Jordaens. But their love of food, drink and revelry is a social phenomenon and goes hand in hand with religious, social and family rituals, some of which go back to early Christian, and even pagan, times. In the whole of Belgium folklore is still very much alive and almost any pretext is good enough for a party, a fête, a procession or a carnival. Such rituals are highly organised and the responsibility of guilds which are as competitive as they are energetic.

These guilds, which are so very much part of Belgian tradition today, are a remnant of the Middle Ages. Then every aspect of life was regulated by them, not least the wine and food trade (the beer trade was mostly in the hands of monasteries). An evocative reminder of this, which also reflects the important role played by food in Belgian life, is the wealth of street names that have something to do with it. Brussels alone has more than 120 streets that are named after some kind of foodstuff, from the Rue du Marché aux Fromages to the Impasse aux Huîtres, from the Vieille Halle aux Blés to the Petite Rue au Beurre.

Like all cuisines, the cooking of the Belgian provinces goes from the simplest country fare to the most sophisticated dishes. It is, however, rarely complicated, for elaboration only came with the inventive cuisine of gastronomes. Good restaurants are thirteen to the dozen in Belgium and it is relatively easy to find excellent versions of a number of regional dishes that have, so to speak, been « standardised » into becoming national dishes — waterzoois of chicken, rabbit or shellfish, carbonnades, choesels, eels with herbs, rabbit with prunes, etc.

When it comes to more genuinely regional specialities, however, the picture changes. Unless they are lucky enough to be guests in a Belgian household in which international cuisine has not stamped out a taste for regional dishes, or to experience a real morsel of rural or provincial life in Belgium, most visitors keen on getting to know more about the cooking of the Flemish and Walloon provinces will either have to try and recreate it for themselves, with the help of recipes, or ferret out the rare restaurants that offer genuine *cuisine du terroir*. It is ironical that a large number of restaurateurs who personally appreciate authentic regional cooking do not think that it will suit the taste of their clientèle. Noël C. Anselot, whose book, *Cuisine en Ardenne, Famenne et Gaume* is a delight to read for all those who are interested in the cookery of that region, relates how once, when he was having lunch in one of the best restaurants in the Ardennes, he asked the *patron* what he himself would be eating that day. It was to be a *potée aux haricots*, a substantial country dish halfway between a soup and a stew in which bacon is cooked with potatoes and green beans and flavoured with cream, vinegar and a lot of pepper. This was far more appealing to the author than the sophisticated game dishes that have made the gastronomic reputation of the Ardennes, and he asked to have some too. It proved delicious. After a memorable meal, the author asked the *patron* why on earth this delicious dish was not on the menu. « Oh, but I simply would not dare ! » was the answer.

The geographical region which, in 1830, became the kingdom of Belgium has been torn by wars and invasions for most of its existence and suffered several centuries of foreign occupation. It is only natural that the Belgians should have developed a certain suspicion of foreigners and a definite resistance to the influence of other cultures. A few traces remain here and there, such as the Penitents' Procession in Veurne, which is a remnant of the Spanish occupation of Flanders, but altogether the resistance has been pretty effective.

The will to preserve a cultural identity has shielded the cuisine of the Belgian provinces, not only from the influence of invading powers but also from that of the Belgian colonies. The colonial experience made a deep impact upon the cuisine of other countries — Britain and the Netherlands in particular. Not so Belgium. But then, Belgium is more attached than most countries to its traditions.

Practically all traditional Belgian dishes are ancient. Many of them can be dated to medieval times and even earlier. Those that feature vegetables such as potatoes, beans or tomatoes, which were brought to Europe from America, often go back to the sixteenth and seventeenth centuries.

It is impossible to describe the cuisine of any country in a few words. The cooking of the Belgian provinces is no exception. There are features that are typical of a particular region or province — in Flanders, for instance, you'll find velvety sauces made with butter, cream and egg yolks, not unlike those of Normandy ; in Limbourg there remains a tradition of cooking with red wine ; in the Ardennes there is a predilection for rich, aromatic brown sauces that go well with game.

Nevertheless, there are certain features that are common to the cooking of most Belgian provinces and may therefore be said to be national characteristics. Some of these — the preponderance of pork dishes, the importance of vegetables or the enormous variety of biscuits, breads and pastries — have an economic and social *raison d'être*. Others, like the taste for sweet-salt or sweet-sour combinations, or the use of beer in cooking, are part of an historical tradition.

Although there are extensive areas of beef breeding in western Flanders, Namur and Liège, it is pork that takes pride of place in Belgian regional cookery. In rural areas, for obvious economic reasons it was, and to some extent still is, the staple meat in a diet that included relatively little else than vegetables and bread. Slaughtering the pig was a big social event in which a whole village might participate. Certain parts of the pig, such as the liver and other offals, were eaten right away and rest was salted and dried, smoked or made into *confits* ; nowadays deep-freezing has replaced many of these traditional ways of preserving meat.

There are literally hundreds of dishes in Belgian cuisine that use pork in some form or other, from the simplest *omelette au lard* to the traditional pressed head of the pig which rates high among the specialities of several provinces, especially those of Antwerp and Namur. None are more famous than the two foremost Belgian hams — those of Flanders and the Ardennes. Both are eaten raw, salted, dried and smoked, but they are quite different in taste, their difference being due to the land the pigs are grazed on. The flat, fertile, well-irrigated pastures of Flanders give a fat, tender, juicy ham which is lightly smoked ; whilst the *sarts* of the Ardennes, hilly moors covered with heather and gorse, give a drier, more aromatic ham, which is smoked in *boucans* (large funnel-shaped chimneys) over tangy juniper wood.

Belgium is not only an agricultural country with a large farming industry but also a nation of kitchen gardeners ; the growing and cooking of vegetables is a matter of pride in rural and urban alike. The list of vegetables to be found in a Belgian market is impressive and includes, among many others, the « national » vegetables, sprouts and chicons (witloofs, or Belgian chicory as the Americans call it — the British know it as Belgian endive), celeriac, kohlrabi, several varieties of beans and cabbages, winter radish, sorrel, tomatoes, asparagus, salsify, peas and mange-tout peas, cauliflowers, turnips, carrots, celery, hopshoots and a large variety of wild mushrooms.

In several provinces you will find a numer of ratatouilles or fricassées of vegetables, sometimes eaten on their own without the addition of meat. Vegetable soups are often closer to stews and versions of the *potée*, a soup-cum-stew of vegetables and bits of pork, are found in every province. It is significant that in the French-speaking provinces one does not say *boire sa soupe* (to drink one's soup) as in France, but *manger sa soupe* (to eat one's soup).

As for potatoes, of which there is a large variety, no book about Belgian cooking should fail to mention the national phenomenon of *frites*, or chips, even though they can in no way qualify as a regional speciality. Suffice it to say that they are the best in the world and that, frowned upon as they are by the more unbending defenders of gastronomy, they have become part of modern Belgian culinary tradition.

It is difficult to trace exactly how this national passion came about, but we find it interesting that the person who was instrumental in helping to spread the culture of the potato in Europe should have been a Flemish botanist, Charles de l'Ecluse (or Carolus Clusius, as he is also known), who was in charge of Maximilian II's gardens in Vienna. De l'Ecluse received a couple of the « divine tubers » in 1588, some thirty years after the vegetable was first brought to Europe from the Americas. He drew them, planted and reproduced them and persuaded the emperor to decree that their culture in Hapsburg lands was of prime importance.

The crowning glory of Belgian cooking is its *pâtisserie*. Recipes for this alone would fill a book the size of the present one. As in other northern European countries, there is a tradition of good bread-baking for a start. But it is the combination of two national traits — a fondness for social and religious rituals and a sweet tooth — that turns this tradition into something closer to genius.

Belgian imagination finds its most lyrical and whimsical expression in the names of regional tarts, cakes and biscuits, from the *Baisers de Malmédy* (Kisses of Malmédy) to the *Pensées troublées d'Arlon* (Troubled Thoughts of Arlon). Unfortunately the origin of these delightful names is often lost in the mists of time and the various interpretations that have been put forward send many a learned gentleman into a frenzy of protest and scholarly quibbling.

As we saw earlier, the Belgians' determination to protect their national and regional patrimony from foreign influence has proved effective. A result of this is that they were virtually untouched by what the historians of gastronomy like to call « the first gastronomic revolution », which took place in the sixteenth century when the arrival in France of a number of brilliant Tuscan cooks, in the retinue of Catherine de' Medici upon her marriage to Henri II, swept the country and, as a result, part of northern Europe had a totally new outlook that was the first step in modern culinary art and the origin of *grande cuisine*.

One of the culinary concepts that this « revolution » did its best to blot out (and which, ironically enough, was recently rediscovered by the exponents of *nouvelle cuisine*) survived undisturbed in Belgian culinary tradition : the combination of sweet-salt or sweet-sour flavours in the same dish. This tradition also exists in other European countries, namely Germany, Austria, Britain, the Netherlands, Scandinavia and Italy (in France, after the sixteenth century and until the advent of *nouvelle cuisine*, it was confined to some pork, duck and game dishes). In Italy the tradition is a direct remnant of Roman taste. Whether the Romans were also responsible for introducing this taste to northern Europe, or whether it developed there spontaneously as it did in Middle and Far Eastern countries, is a moot point. We do know that in northern Europe it goes as far back as one can trace it, to the early Middle Ages.

The most common way of achieving a sweet-salt flavour is by adding fruit to meat or fish. In Belgium as in other northern European countries, certain meats or fish seem to call for certain fruits : pork for apples or prunes, duck for oranges or cherries, sole for grapes, salt fish for apples, rabbit for prunes, pheasant for cranberries or chestnuts, and so on. In winter, when fresh fruit was not readily available, cooks resorted to dried fruit. Sultanas, prunes and other dried fruit such as apricots were imported from Portugal and the Levant as far back as the thirteenth century and still feature in a large number of Belgian dishes. Despite the greater availability of fruit in winter, the tradition of using dried fruits in certain dishes persists. There is, for instance, a delicious way of cooking dried pears with bacon that comes from the province of Limbourg (recipe page no 179).

Honey, too, was used to sweeten certain meat or fish dishes until the thirteenth century, when cane sugar was first introduced from the Levant in the wake of the Crusaders. Sourness was obtained from vinegar, verjuice (the juice of unripe fruit — sour green apples, crab apples, sour grapes, etc.) or the addition of beer, its bitterness always counteracted by sugar or fruit. Sometimes the fruit was part of the beer itself ; a remnant of this can be found in *Kriek*, a lambic beer in which cherries are macerated.

The use of beer in Belgian cooking is very ancient, possibly even pre-medieval. Before hops were added in the early Middle Ages, *cervoise*, an ale made from fermented cereals, was used. It is interesting to note here that the English words « beer », « hop » and « malt » are of Flemish origin.

Wine and spices were imported into the area that later became Belgium as far back as Roman times. Of wine cookery, an important tradition remains in the province of Limbourg. From time immemorial spices were used to preserve meat, fish and vegetables and to mask the taste of food that had gone off. In the Middle Ages the spice trade broke all records (in England and other countries rents could be paid in peppercorns), but it started to decline after the seventeenth century.

Belgian cooking does not make use of a large variety of spices. Insofar as any spice may be called the « national » spice of Belgium, though in this case the appellation is due more to its indiscriminate use than to its actual flavouring, it is nutmeg. You will find it in a huge number of dishes, from soups to carbonnades. Less often used, but so much more effective that it should be placed above nutmeg in the list of « Belgian » spices (it is in fact the only spice that is actually native to Belgium), is juniper. The berries, which are also used to flavour genever, a strong spirit that resembles gin and is known as *pèkèt* in Wallonia, characterise the cooking of Liège and the Ardennes. Saffron was brought to Belgium by the Romans and, like other spices, was much used in medieval cookery. A traditional ingredient of fish soups and stews in Mediterranean countries, it is still used in Belgium in a delicious mussel soup (possibly one of the few remnants of Spanish influence in Flemish cooking) and in a few sweets such as the beloved *Rijstpap* of Flanders. Ginger, cloves, cinnamon and vanilla are used to flavour a large number of biscuits and sweets (the most notable being *speculoos*) and also occasionally find their way into stews.

Herbs play an important role in Belgian cooking, though their variety is relatively limited. Some, like thyme, come from southern Europe, but most of the others are native to Belgium, or became so after the Romans introduced them to this part of the world. This is the case for chervil, the « national » herb without which a number of dishes, many of them Flemish, would be unthinkable. Parsley, chives and tarragon are close runners-up. Sage figures in many pork dishes.

Garlic is used sparingly in native Belgian cookery, with some glaring exceptions such as the famous goose dish from Visé which makes use of no less than two whole heads of it. On the other hand shallots and, of course, onions are used, together or separately, to flavour an enormous number of dishes, but never in the abandoned way that characterises the cookery of southern European countries.

Finally, a word about Belgian cheeses. Almost every province has one or several representative cheeses : Brabant has hettekees, stinkkees (which, as its name implies, is strong), schopkees, pottekees ; Liège its numerous and well-known herves and maquêyes ; Flanders the Westfleteren and Watou cheeses ; Limbourg the wittekaas, boerenplattekaas and Limburger ; Hainaut the Chimay, the boulettes de Beaumont ; Namur its famous cassettes and boulettes, the Maredsous, Romedenne, Couvin, Culdes-Sarts, Surice and Floreffe and Belgian Luxembourg its crottes and the goat cheeses of Menufontaine.

Some of these cheeses were started by monks in the Middle Ages — among them, Chimay and the abdijkaas of Limbourg were the work of Trappists, Maredsous that of Benedictines.

The famous cheese made on the Herve plateau in the province of Liège was it seems, one of the first cheeses to be widely distributed in Europe in the Renaissance, and that because of the role played by Jews in its making. The Jews had a rule that they could only eat cheese made by, or in the presence of, another Jew, so the Herve cheese-makers decided to employ a number of Jews on their farms. Soon the cheeses were exported elsewhere in Europe where there were Jewish communities and so became well known outside their region of origin.

WINE, BEER AND OTHER DRINKS

Wine used to be grown in Belgium, especially in the Liège region, but the industrial revolution and vine diseases soon put paid to that. The last commercial vineyards disappeared soon after the Second World War. Here and there you will still find a small private vineyard and recently an attempt was made to replant vineyards in several areas, including Torgny, in Gaume, where the climate is relatively mild. A little wine also is made from the grapes grown in the hothouses of Hoeilaart, Duisburg and Overijse, but what « local » wine there is in Belgium comes from neighbouring Luxembourg and more specifically from the valley of the Moselle Luxembourgeoise.

Beer, the national drink of Belgium, needs no introduction. Suffice it to say that there is a seemingly endless variety of beers and that the average Belgian drinks over 150 litres of it a year. There are two types of beer : low-fermentation, pils-type pale ales, such as Stella-Artois ; and high-fermentation beers, such as the famous Trappist beers and stouts which were originally brewed in Cistercian monasteries. The best-known amongst them are those of Chimay, Orval, St Sixtus, Westmalle and Rochefort.

Very special beers are also made in the region of Brussels ; they are *lambic*, a strong beer made from a mixture of wheat and barley, and *gueuze*, which is a one or two-year old bottled lambic. A make of gueuze is the aptly-named *Mort Subite* (Sudden Death). Another interesting lambic beer is *Kriek*, which owes its fruity flavour and red colour to cherries which are traditionally macerated in it. Faro, another Brussels beer made mostly from wheat, is very ancient.

Other drinks include cider, which is made in several provinces, including Eastern Flanders, Liège and Belgian Luxembourg ; *cervoise*, an ale originally flavoured with ginger but now tasting of juniper ; *hydromel* (mead) ; a number of eaux-de-vie of fruit, like the blackcurrant eau-de-vie of Vielsalm ; fruit liqueurs such as the strawberry liqueur made at Wépion, the centre of the strawberry-growing region ; the famous pine-flavoured Elixir de Spa and its cousin the Elixir d'Anvers, which tastes a little like Bénédictine. Finally, no list of Belgian regional drinks, however brief, would be complete without a mention of Maitrank (May Drink), a delicious spring wine cup with the distinctive flavour of sweet woodruff.

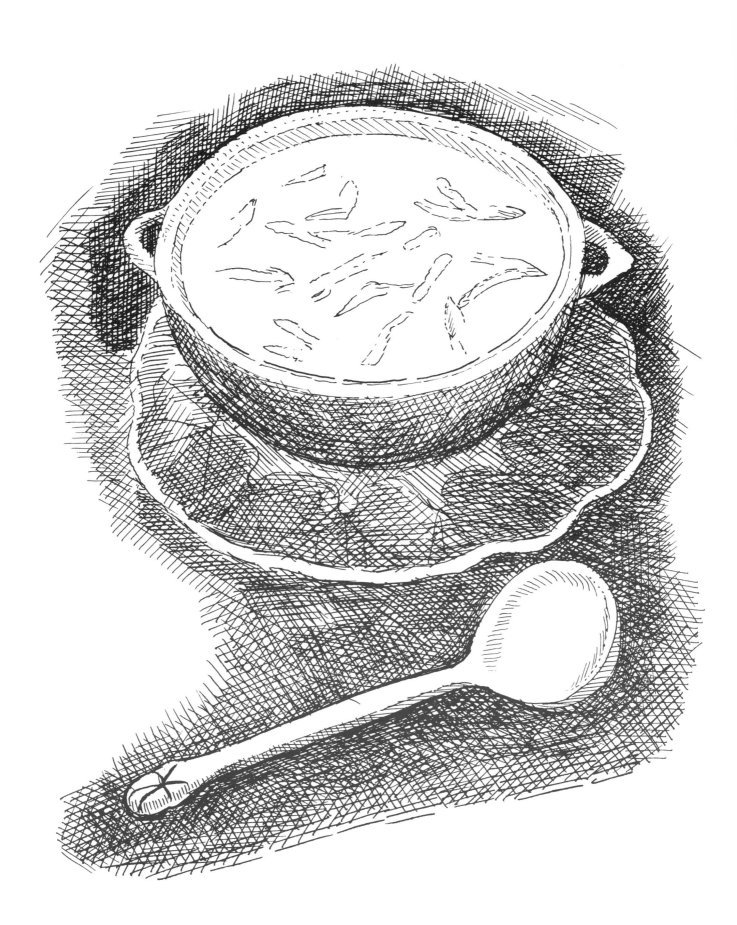

soups

POTÉE D'ANGUILLES

More of a stew than a soup of eels and mussels. from Flanders

1 kg 500 g. eels
150 g. smoked bacon
6 large onions
300 g. shelled mussels
1/2 l. dry white wine
1 1/2 l. water

1 kg potatoes
2 tbsp. tomato purée
grated peel of one orange
bouquet garni* (bay leaf, sprig thyme,
    clove garlic)
salt, pepper

- In the olive oil, gently brown the thinly sliced onions and bacon, cut into small strips, for 5 minutes.
- Add the flour and orange peel, cook for a further 3 minutes or until the flour begins to brown.
- Add the white wine and reduce to half its original quantity over a fairly high heat.
- Add the water and peeled and chopped potatoes (approximately 1-inch cubes), the bouquet garni and season lightly with salt.
- Simmer for about 10 minutes or until the potatoes are almost cooked.
- Add the eels, cut into pieces about 2 inches long, the fresh shelled mussels and the tomato purée. Season with pepper to taste and gently simmer for about 15 minutes.
- Serve with plenty of garlic bread.

This serves 6 people.

* All asterisks refer you to the Glossary at the back of the book.

POTAGE AUX HUÎTRES

An expensive but delicious oyster soup, from Flanders

2 dozen oysters
60 g. butter
2 tbsp. flour
3/4 l. hot milk or veal stock (see p. 183)
3/4 tsp. anchovy essence

nutmeg
cayenne pepper
1 dl. double cream
juice of 1 lemon
salt, pepper

- Clean and open the oysters, discarding the shells but reserving the liquor.
- Melt butter in a large saucepan, stir in flour and cook gently for 2 to 3 minutes. Add milk or stock gradually so that the mixture remains smooth. Season to taste with the anchovy essence, nutmeg and cayenne pepper. Add the cream and simmer for 15 minutes.
- Just before you are ready to serve, add the oysters and their liquor, heat them through ; this should take about 2 to 3 minutes. Don't overcook, oysters become tough if overcooked ; they are ready when they begin to curl at the edges.
- Adjust the seasoning with salt and pepper. Add the lemon juice to sharpen the flavour and more cayenne and nutmeg if liked.
- Pour into warm soup bowls and sprinkle with parsley. Don't wait for latecomers, as the oysters carry on cooking in the hot liquid.

CRÈME DE CREVETTES

A delicious soup of shrimps, cream and brandy, from Flanders

500 g. shrimps
    (fresh, with shells, and
    the bigger the better)
1 onion
1 stick or celery
1 carrot   } finely chopped
1 leek
3 large tomatoes, peeled & seeded
2 dl. cream
1 egg yolk

1 l. water
2 glasses dry white wine
1 small glass brandy
bouquet garni* (thyme, bay leaf,
    2 stalks parsley, clove of garlic)
60 g. butter
30 g. flour

- Melt 30 g. of butter in a large saucepan and gently cook the finely chopped vegetables over a low heat, without browning, for about 10 minutes.

- Shell the shrimps, reserving the shells and heads.

- Add the shells and heads of shrimps to vegetables, pour a litre of hot water into the saucepan, add the bouquet garni and tomatoes. Season with pepper, but no salt at this stage as the shrimp shells and heads may be salty enough.

- Simmer gently in a covered saucepan for 1 hour.

- Pour the stock through a sieve, pressing the vegetables and shells with a wooden spoon to extract all the juice.

- Melt the rest of the butter in the saucepan, add the flour and make a roux*. Stirring constantly, add the vegetable and shrimp stock in a steady stream and bring to the boil. Simmer gently for 15 minutes.

- Beat the egg yolk and cream together. Away from the heat, stir in the egg and cream mixture.

- Add the shrimps and brandy.

- Return the saucepan to a very low heat, stir gently until the soup thickens slightly and the shrimps are cooked (this should take just 2 to 3 minutes).

  Don't let the soup boil or it may curdle.

SOUPE À LA BIÈRE DOUCE

An unusual soup made from sweet brown ale

1 l. sweet brown ale (stout)
1/2 l. milk
2 egg yolks
1/2 stick cinnamon

1 tsp. powdered ginger
1 tbsp. cornflour
3 tbsp. cold water
salt
rind of 1 lemon

- Simmer the beer with the lemon rind, cinnamon and ginger for 10 minutes.
- Mix the cornflour and cold water together to a smooth paste. Add a few spoonfuls of the hot beer and then add the cornflour mixture to the beer in the saucepan.
- Cook the soup gently for a further 10 minutes.
- Mix the egg yolks and milk together and, away from the heat, add to the soup in the saucepan. Heat through thoroughly without boiling and serve with slices of fried bread.

Bathers on a Flemish beach

POTAGE AU CRESSON

Cream of watercress soup from Limbourg

2 bunches watercress
1 large onion
1 leek
500 g. potatoes

1 1/2 l. chicken stock
1 dl. cream
30 g. butter
salt, pepper

- Chop the onion and the white of the leek and sauté in butter in a large saucepan, for 2 to 3 minutes.
- Peel and chop the potatoes. Roughly chop the leaves and tender stalks of the watercress.
- Add watercress, potatoes and the stock to the saucepan. Bring to the boil and simmer for 45 minutes.
- Liquidise, return soup to saucepan, season to taste with salt and pepper. Add the cream, cook for a further 3 minutes and serve.

POTAGE AUX CAROTTES

A creamy carrot soup from Brussels

500 g. carrots
500 g. potatoes
3/4 l. chicken stock
1/2 l. milk

1 dl. cream
30 g. butter
2 tbsp. chopped parsley
salt, pepper

- Melt the butter in a large saucepan and gently cook the peeled and sliced carrots and potatoes, without browning, for 10 minutes.
- Add the hot chicken stock. Cover and simmer for 20 to 25 minutes.
- Liquidise. Add milk, season to taste and simmer gently for a further 10 minutes.
- Stir in the cream and serve with a sprinkling of parsley.

The last barge-horse on the Ourthe, 1929

SOUPE AU POTIRON

Pumpkin soup, from Hainaut

1 kg pumpkin
500 g. potatoes
1 l. water
1/2 l. milk
bouquet garni* (sprig thyme, bay leaf,
    2 cloves garlic, parsley stalk)

50 g. vermicelle
30 g. butter
salt
freshly-milled black pepper

- Peel and cut into small cubes the pumpkin and potatoes. Place them in a large saucepan and cover with the water. The water should just cover the pumpkin and potatoes, so add or subtract from the litre suggested.
- Add the bouquet garni and 1/2 teaspoon salt. Bring to the boil and simmer covered for 1 hour.
- Add the milk and simmer for a further 10 minutes.
- Liquidise. Add the cooked vermicelle and simmer for a further 2 minutes to heat the vermicelle.
- Just before serving, stir in 30 g. of butter cut into small pieces and check seasoning by adding a few twists of freshly ground black pepper.

POTAGE DE POIREAUX AUX TOMATES

An unusual soup of tomatoes and leeks, from the Namur region

8 leeks
4 large tomatoes
250 g. potatoes
1 l. water
bouquet garni* (thyme, clove garlic,
    piece of lemon peel)

1 dl. cream
2 tbsp. parsley or chervil
salt, pepper

- Chop the white part only (reserving the green part) of the leeks very finely. Peel, seed and roughly chop the tomatoes.
- Melt the butter in a saucepan, add the chopped leeks and tomatoes, gently cook over a very low heat. This should be done in a covered saucepan, the vegetables should not take on any colour and this very gentle sweating of the vegetables can take up to 30 to 45 minutes.
- While this is happening, chop the green part of the leeks, discarding any very tough-looking leaves, put them in a saucepan and add the peeled and chopped potatoes. Cover the leeks and potatoes with a litre of water, add the bouquet garni and season to taste with salt and pepper. Bring to the boil and simmer for 30 to 40 minutes.
- Remove the green leek leaves and the bouquet garni. Liquidise the potato and stock mixture together. Return to the saucepan, bring to the boil and add the tomato and leek mixture. Cook for a further 10 minutes.
- Stir in the cream and serve with a sprinkling of parsley or chervil.

Market day at Charleroi

CONSOMMÉ DES FLANDRES

A thin vegetable soup made with chicken stock

1 l. good chicken stock (see p. 182)
1 big carrot
1 medium-sized turnip
1 onion
1 leek

250 g. shelled peas
4 tbsp. chopped parsley
30 g. butter
salt, pepper

- Chop very finely the carrot, turnip, leek and onion.
- Melt the butter in a large saucepan and gently sauté the vegetables for 10 minutes without browning them.
- Add the chicken stock and bring to the boil, season to taste. Simmer for 20 minutes.
- Add the peas and cook for a further 10 minutes, or until the peas are just cooked.
- Pour into a soup tureen, sprinkle with parsley and serve with crusty French bread.

CONSOMMÉ DE BETTERAVES

A refreshing summer soup made from beetroot, from the Ardennes

750 g. raw beetroot, peeled and
    chopped
10 large spring onions, chopped
1 1/2 l. water
1 cucumber
1 tbsp. red wine vinegar

1 tbsp. lemon juice
bouquet garni* (bay leaf, sprig thyme,
    piece lemon rind, clove garlic)
1 dl. sour cream
2 tbsp. chopped chives
salt and freshly-milled pepper

- Put the prepared beetroot and chopped spring onions in a large saucepan with the water and the bouquet garni. Bring to the boil, simmer gently uncovered for about 1 hour. The beetroot will have lost its redness and have a pale look about it.
- Peel and dice the cucumber, add to the soup and simmer for a further 15 minutes.
- Place a large sieve over your serving bowl. Pour the soup through the sieve and leave for 10 minutes to allow all the consommé to drain through.
- To sharpen the taste, add the vinegar and lemon juice. Season with salt and freshly milled pepper.
- Chill well and serve with a dribble of sour cream and a sprinkling of chopped chives.

Flemish lace-maker

SOUPE TCHANTCHÈS

A vegetable soup, from Liège

4 sticks celery
2 leeks
1 onion
500 g. potatoes
1 dl. milk

60 g. butter
100 g. sorrel
100 g. chervil
1 l. chicken stock (see p. 182)
50 g. vermicelle
salt, pepper

- Chop the whites of the leeks, celery and onions and sauté in 30 g. of butter for 5 minutes, without browning, in a large saucepan.
- Add the chopped potatoes and stock, bring to the boil and simmer for 45 minutes.
- In the meantime, finely chop the sorrel and chervil and gently cook in 30 g. of butter for 10 to 15 minutes. Don't brown or overcook.
- Liquidise the soup ; return to the saucepan. Add herbs, vermicelle and milk, season with salt and pepper. Simmer for a further 10 minutes or until the vermicelle is cooked and serve in warmed soup bowls.

A street singer, Liège

POTÉE PAYSANNE

A vegetable and bacon soup from Liège

200 g. piece lean bacon
2 leeks
2 sticks celery
small white cabbage

3 potatoes
2 l. water or chicken stock
1 clove garlic
salt, pepper

- Chop the leeks, celery and potatoes roughly ; place them in a large saucepan and cover with water or stock.
- Remove any tough leaves from the cabbage, cut into 4 and remove centre stalk, roughly chop and add to saucepan.
- Add the piece of bacon and crushed garlic, season with pepper (no salt at this stage as the bacon may be salty enough) and bring to the boil.
- Simmer for 1 1/2 hours. Remove the bacon and dice. Using a balloon whisk, pound the soup ; this thickens the soup but leaves most of the vegetables in a recognisable form.
- Serve with the bacon, very hot, and with slices of fried bread.

« Botrèsses » (coal-carriers) from the province of Liège

starters

ASPERGES AUX CREVETTES

A delicate herb-flavoured hors d'œuvre, from Flanders

1 kg. asparagus
2 eggs
1 tbsp. mixed fresh herbs (chervil,
    parsley, chives, tarragon), chopped
juice of 1 lemon

1 dl. cream
1 tbsp. French mustard
    (tarragon flavoured if possible)
salt, pepper
150 g. small shrimps

GARNISH

4 large prawns, whole
thin slices of lemon

- Fill a very large saucepan with water, salt it and bring it to the boil.
- Wash, trim and peel the asparagus, and cut off the hard ends. Tie them in bundles and cook them for 15-20 minutes in boiling water, or steam them for about 25 minutes. (They should be firm, not limp.)
- Hardboil the eggs for 10 minutes, put them in cold water and shell them. Then chop them up finely.
- When the asparagus are done, drain well and arrange on a serving dish. Allow to cool.
- In a bowl, mix the herbs, cream, mustard, lemon juice and chopped eggs, season with salt and pepper and add the shrimps.
- Spoon the shrimp sauce over the asparagus, garnish with prawns and thinly sliced lemon and serve very cold.

ROULADES D'ASPERGES À L'ARDENNAISE

Asparagus and Ardennes ham, a good combination

12 thin asparagus
1 tbsp. chopped parsley
1 tbsp. chopped chives
1/2 tbsp. chopped tarragon
2 eggs

1 tbsp. mayonnaise
1 tsp. French mustard
4 large thin slices
    Ardennes ham

GARNISH
mustard cress
chopped parsley
gherkins

hardboiled egg
tomatoes

- Fill a large saucepan with water, salt it and bring it to the boil.
- Wash, trim and peel the asparagus and cut them about 5 inches from the tip. Tie them in two bundles and cook them for about 15 minutes in boiling water. Test the bottoms with a skewer and when they are done, take them out carefully and drain on a napkin, and allow them to cool thoroughly.
- Hardboil the eggs and shell them in cold water, then take out the yolks and work them into a paste with the mayonnaise, mustard and chopped herbs. Check the seasoning carefully.
- Spread each slice of Ardennes ham with a little of the egg mixture, place 3 asparagus tips in each slice and roll the ham around them. Arrange the roulades* in a serving dish.
- Mince the hardboiled egg whites, mix them with some chopped parsley and sprinkle the roulades with it. Garnish with gherkins and mustard cress, slices of hardboiled eggs and quartered tomatoes.

HACHIS DE POIREAUX

A cold hors d'œuvre of leeks and eggs

1 kg. leeks
1 tbsp. olive oil
juice of 1 lemon
2 eggs

1 tbsp. mayonnaise
1 teaspoon French mustard
a few capers

- Trim off the green parts of the leeks, chop up the white part and wash thoroughly, then drain well and pat dry.
- In a saucepan heat 2 tbsp. olive oil and stew the chopped leeks gently for about 8-10 minutes or until cooked.
- Meanwhile hardboil the eggs.
- Put the leeks in a shallow dish, dress them with the lemon juice, salt and pepper and allow to cool.
- Shell the eggs and mash them with a fork, adding the mayonnaise and mustard. Mix in the capers.
- Spread the egg paste onto the leeks and chill for at least 2 hours.

SALADE DE PLEUROTES MIMOSA

A fresh lemon-flavoured salad of oyster mushrooms

500 g pleurotes*
   (oyster mushrooms)
3 eggs
1 shallot

1 tbsp. chopped parsley
juice of 2 lemons
6 tbsp. olive oil
salt, pepper

- First hardboil the eggs for 10 minutes. Place them in cold water and shell them, then separate the whites from the yolks and mince the whites finely with the shallot and parsley. Season with the lemon juice and 4 tbsp. olive oil, salt and pepper.
- Clean the oyster mushrooms, cut into bite-sized chunks and sauté them gently in 2 tbsp. olive oil for 5 minutes.
- Remove the mushrooms to a salad bowl and while they are still warm, add the sauce and marinate the mixture for at least 1 hour.
- Just before serving, mince the egg yolks finely and sprinkle them over the salad.

GÂTEAU D'OIE

A goose pâté en croûte, slightly extravagant to make, but worth the cost and effort

1 small goose
250 g. good quality sausage meat
4 shallots
1 dl. dry white wine
1/2 dl. cognac

salt, pepper
nutmeg
3 crushed juniper berries
1 egg

FOR THE PASTRY

500 g. flour
20 g. yeast
3 eggs
100 g. butter

pinch of salt
1 tbsp. sugar
1 dl. milk

- Skin the goose carefully, in one piece if possible, and reserve the skin.
- Bone the goose completely and mince its flesh with its liver, the sausage meat and the shallots. Add the white wine and cognac, the salt, pepper and spices.
- Knead the mixture thoroughly in a bowl, cover it with the goose skin and stand for 24 hours in a cool place.
- The next day, make the pastry : put the flour in a bowl, make a well and in it put the yeast, diluted with a little milk. Work the yeast with about 1/4 of the flour until you have obtained a soft dough. Cover it with the rest of the flour and let it rise for 1/2 hour.
- When the dough has risen, add the eggs, the butter, a pinch of salt, the sugar and the milk. Knead briskly, cover it with a cloth and put in a warm place to rise for 2 hours.
- Roll out the pastry in a rectangular shape, about 1 centimetre thick, cover this as evenly as possible with the goose skin and wrap the stuffing in the double envelope, shaping it into a rectangular block. Pinch the dough at the edges and place the gâteau on an oiled cake tin, cover with a cloth and stand for another 30 minutes.
- Beat the egg lightly and with a pastry brush paint the whole of the exposed surface of the gâteau with it. With a knife, make a couple of long incisions on the top so as to let air in, and bake the gâteau in the centre of a preheated oven at medium temperature for 45-50 minutes.
- This gâteau may be served hot or cold.

SALADE DE PISSENLITS AU LARD

A classic salad, from Liège

4 medium potatoes
300 g. dandelion leaves
2 shallots
200 g. smoked bacon in one piece

3 tbsp. olive oil
1 1/2 tbsp. red wine vinegar
salt, pepper

- Cook the potatoes in salted boiling water for 20-25 minutes.
- Meanwhile wash and dry the dandelion leaves, chop the shallots finely and dice the bacon.
- Gently sauté the diced bacon in a frying pan in its own fat until crisp and golden.
- Warm a salad bowl.
- When the potatoes are cooked, drain, peel and dice them, then add them to the dandelions in the warm salad bowl with the bacon, the chopped shallots, the olive oil, salt and pepper. Toss carefully.
- Boil quickly 1 1/2 tbsp. vinegar in the bacon fat in the pan and pour over the salad.
- Serve at once.

SALADE LIÉGEOISE

A warm cooked salad of green beans, potatoes and bacon

500 g. haricots princesses or
    green beans
3 large potatoes
125 g. smoked streaky bacon
    in one piece

15 g. butter
1 tbsp. chopped parsley
1 tbsp. chopped spring onions
0.5 dl. red wine vinegar

- Trim and wash the beans and cook them in boiling, salted water. They must remain firm.
- At the same time, cook the potatoes in their skins in boiling salted water.
- While the vegetables are cooking, dice the bacon and fry in 15 g. butter until it changes colour.
- When the potatoes are cooked, peel them and cut them into round. Drain the beans.
- Put the beans in a salad bowl, arrange the potatoes all around, sprinkle with the chopped parsley and spring onions and pour the diced bacon and its fat over the lot.
- Pour the wine vinegar in the frying pan and boil, scraping the bacon juices until the liquid has reduced considerably. Pour over the salad and serve warm.

The needlework lesson, overleaf

SALADE DU PÊCHEUR

A Flemish fisherman's salad of white beans, potatoes and kippers

250 g. dried white beans
1 onion
1 sprig savory
250 g. potatoes
2 cooked beetroots
4 kipper fillets

1 dl. mayonnaise
1 tsp. French mustard
1 shallot
1 tbsp. chopped parsley
4 gherkins

- Soak the beans overnight.
- The next day, put the beans in boiling salted water with the onion cut in two and the savory. When they are cooked but still firm, drain them and remove the onion and savory.
- Cook the potatoes in boiling salted water, peel and dice them. Dice the beetroot.
- Cut the kipper fillets into 1-inch strips and mix them in a salad bowl with the potatoes, beans and beetroot.
- Chop the shallot, parsley and gherkins and mix them into the mayonnaise and mustard. Spoon the sauce over the salad and mix carefully.

Flemish fisherman

CROÛTES OSTENDAISES

Shrimps on toast Ostend-style

4 slices of white bread
50 g. butter
2 tbsp. groundnut oil
1 tbsp. flour
2.5 dl. milk

1 egg yolk
100 g. small peeled shrimps
60 g. grated Swiss cheese
salt, pepper

- Cut the crusts from the slices of bread and fry them in a mixture of 2 tbsp. oil and 25 g. butter, then keep them warm on an oven tin.
- Make a roux* with 25 g. butter and a tbsp. flour, adding the milk to make a thick béchamel (see p. 184). Away from the heat add the shrimps and 50 g. cheese, and mix well. Check the seasoning.
- Spread the shrimp mixture on the croûtes, sprinkle with a little more grated cheese, and place in a hot oven until the cheese is golden all over.

CROQUETTES DE MOULES FLAMANDES

Fried mussel patties, a welcome alternative to the ubiquitous shrimp croquettes of Belgian restaurants

1 kg. mussels
1.5 dl. dry white wine
2 shallots, chopped
2 sprigs parsley
1 celery heart
1 onion
60 g. butter
1 tbsp. flour

2 dl. milk
3 eggs
juice of 1 lemon
salt, pepper
flour
breadcrumbs
peanut oil

- Scrape and clean the mussels thoroughly (see page 69), then put them in a wide, deep pan with the wine, shallots and parsley. Cook over medium heat until all the mussels have opened.
- Drain the mussels when they have cooled down a little, but reserve the liquid. Shell them and chop them finely.
- Chop the onion and celery finely and cook them gently in 30 g. butter until translucent.
- Strain the mussel liquid, add 2 tbsp. of it to the vegetables and simmer until all the liquid has evaporated.
- In another pan, make a roux* with 30 g. butter and 1 tbsp. flour, add 1 dl. of the mussel liquid and 2 dl. warm milk and cook, stirring with a wooden spoon, until the sauce is smooth and thick.
- Add the chopped mussels, onion and celery to the sauce and beat in gradually 3 egg yolks and the lemon juice.
- Check the seasoning, bring gently to the boil, then turn off the heat and let the mixture cool a little.
- Pour the mixture onto a cold slab or a very large flat plate, allow to go thoroughly cold, then cut the paste into egg-sized bits.
- Beat the egg whites until very stiff.
- Roll each egg-sized bit of paste in your hands and shape into oval patties. Roll these in flour, dip them into the egg whites, roll them in breadcrumbs and fry in oil until golden and crisp.

Female shrimpers at Middelkerke

QUENELLES DE LA MÈRE FRANÇOISE

A dish from Brussels : quenelles of herring and salmon

100 g. fresh, soft white
    breadcrumbs
1 dl. milk
3 eggs
2 shallots
30 g. butter

50 g. mushroom caps
1 tbsp. chopped parsley
1/2 tbsp. chopped tarragon
4 smoked herring fillets
25 g. smoked salmon
salt, pepper

- Soak the breadcrumbs in the milk for a few minutes, then press to remove excess milk. Beat the eggs.
- Put the breadcrumbs in a bowl and gradually beat in the three eggs.
- Chop the shallots finely and cook them until transparent in 30 g. butter. Chop the mushrooms finely and add them to the shallots. Cook for 2-3 minutes then add the herbs.
- Fold the vegetables into the breadcrumb mixture.
- Chop the herring fillets and the smoked salmon and add them to the mixture. Season carefully with salt and pepper.
- Shape a dollop of the mixture into a small sausage and poach in boiling water to see whether it will hold together. If the mixture is still too liquid or soft, beat in a little flour, then shape the rest of the mixture into quenelles or sausages.
- Poach these in lightly salted boiling water for 1 or 2 minutes, drain carefully and serve very hot with a herbal or shallot butter.

MOUSSE DE TRUITE FUMÉE

A delicate smoky-flavoured mousse with a watercress sauce

4 smoked trout fillets
30 g. butter
1 tbsp. flour
2 shallots
1 dl. dry white wine
1.5 dl. milk
1 dstp. powdered gelatine
2 tbsp. cream
salt, pepper
nutmeg

GARNISH

watercress
1 lemon

WATERCRESS SAUCE

1 large bunch watercress
1 shallot
25 g. butter
juice of 1/2 lemon
salt, pepper
0.5 dl. thick cream
1 tbsp. chopped chives

- Chop the shallots and cook them gently in the butter until soft, then add the flour and moisten with the wine, stirring all the time until the alcohol has evaporated. Add the milk gradually then stir in the gelatine.
- Pour this into the liquidiser, flake in the trout fillets and blend at high speed to obtain a smooth mixture.
- Remove the mixture into a bowl, add the cream and season to taste with salt, pepper and a little grated nutmeg.
- Pour into a jelly or fish-shaped mould and chill for at least 6 hours.
- Meanwhile make the watercress sauce : chop the shallot, wash and chop the watercress and stew them together, covered, in the butter for 8-10 minutes.
- Put the watercress into a liquidiser and blend until smooth.
- Add the cream, lemon juice, chives, salt and pepper to taste, pour into a sauceboat and chill.
- Before serving, unmould the mousse, decorate it with sprigs of watercress and lemon wedges and serve the sauce separately.

TERRINE DE LIÈVRE À LA LIÉGEOISE

A hare pâté with the distinctive flavour of juniper berries

1 hare
500 g. mixed minced meat
    (1/3 veal, 2/3 fat pork)
125 g. fat bacon in one piece
1 onion
2 shallots
25 g. butter
0.5 dl. brandy

6 crushed juniper berries
1/4 tsp. thyme
1 crushed bayleaf
6 peppercorns
salt, pepper
200 g. back pork fat
    (or fat bacon if back
    fat is not available)

- Strip all the meat from the hare and mince it.
- Cut the fat bacon into small dices and mix it with the minced hare, veal and pork.
- Chop the onion and shallots finely. Sauté them gently in butter until transparent, then add them to the meat.
- Add the brandy, crushed juniper berries, peppercorns and herbs, season carefully with salt and pepper and knead well to mix the ingredients thoroughly.
- Cut the back fat into very thin strips and line a terrine with them. Half fill it with the minced meat, cover the mixture with another layer of fat strips and add the remaining meat. Arrange the rest of the fat strips across the top of the pâté.
- Place the terrine in a baking tin filled with water and cook uncovered in a slowish oven for 1 1/2 hours. The pâté is cooked when it starts to come away from the sides of the dish.

FLAMICHE AUX CHICONS

A dish from the Brabant : a chicory and cream cheese flan, delicious hot or cold

FOR THE PASTRY

200 g. flour
8 g. yeast
1 dl. milk
30 g. butter
1 egg
1/4 tsp. salt

FOR THE FILLING

400 g. chicons (chicory)
30 g. butter
100 g. cream cheese
2 eggs
1 dl. double cream
salt, pepper

- First prepare the pastry : dilute the yeast in warmed milk and melt the butter. Sift the flour in a large bowl and add gradually the milk and yeast mixture and melted butter. Beat in the egg and salt. Knead the dough vigorously, shape it into a ball, wrap it in greaseproof paper and leave it to rise in a warmish place for 2 hours.
- Meanwhile chop the chicons finely and stew them gently in 30 g. butter for about 10 minutes.
- In a bowl, whisk the eggs with the cream, add the cream cheese and season with salt and pepper.
- Roll out the pastry fairly thin, line a flan tin with it and prick the surface with a fork.
- Spread the chicons over the pastry and pour the cream mixture over them.
- Cook in a moderately hot oven for 15-20 minutes or until the flan has set and browned.

TOURTE ARDENNAISE

A comforting cold-weather dish — a pie of pork, chestnuts and apple

FOR THE PASTRY

125 g. plain flour	salt
120 g. butter	water
1 egg	

FOR THE FILLING

3 cooking apples	25 g. butter
1 tin chestnuts au naturel	1 dl. port (or madeira)
200 g. lean pork meat, minced	salt, pepper
2 eggs	

- First make the pastry : sieve the flour in a large bowl and make a well in the middle. Put in the butter cut in small pieces, the egg and a good pinch of salt. Work quickly together with the fingertips, then add just enough water to make the dough moist. Shape the dough into a ball, put it on a floured board and flatten it with the heel of your palm. Then shape it into a ball once more and repeat the process. Finally, shape it again, wrap it in a greaseproof paper and put it in a cool place for 2 hours.

- Preheat the oven to a moderately hot temperature.

- Peel and core the apples and slice them finely ; drain the tinned chestnuts and chop them up roughly.

- In a bowl, mix thoroughly but delicately the minced pork, the apples, the chestnuts, the port and one egg. Season with salt and plenty of freshly ground black pepper.

- Break the second egg into a small bowl and beat it lightly with a fork.

- Butter the pie dish.

- Roll out two-thirds of the dough into a round shape about 5 millimetres thick and slightly larger in diameter than the pie dish, and line the dish with it, pricking the bottom with a fork.

- Spread the filling into this.

- Roll out the remaining dough in a round shape with the same diameter as the pie dish and cover the pie with it, pinching the pastry edges together.

- With a pastry brush dipped in the beaten egg, paint the whole surface of the pie and make a couple of long incisions on it to let the air in.

- Cook the tourte in a moderately hot oven for 45 minutes and serve hot.

Walloon butter-seller

50

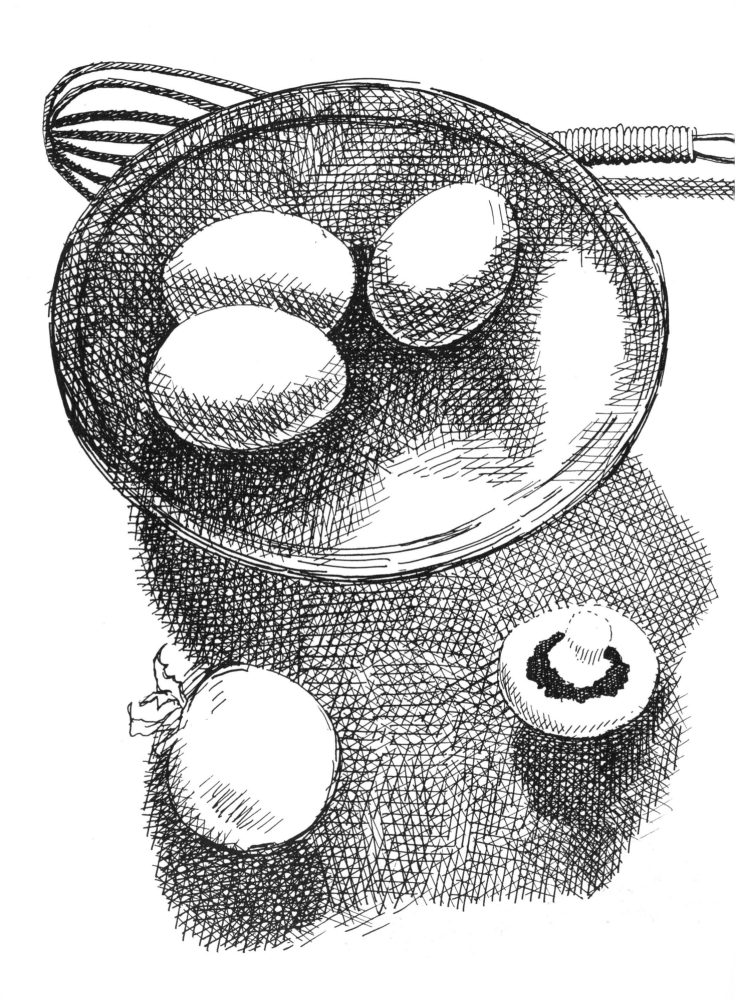

eggs

ŒUFS MEULEMEESTER

An old classic from Bruges

4 eggs
125 g. raw peeled prawns
30 g. butter
1 tbsp. Dijon mustard
1 tbsp. chopped parsley

1 tbsp. chopped chervil
3 dl. cream
salt, pepper
25 g. grated Emmenthal or Gruyère

- Boil the eggs for 7 minutes exactly.
- Plunge them into cold water and shell them.
- While they are still warm and soft, chop them.
- Melt the butter in a pan and add the chopped eggs.
- Add the mustard, herbs and prawns.
- Stir gently, season to taste with salt and freshly ground black pepper and add the cream, shaking the pan to mix them.
- Butter a gratin dish and pour in the mixture.
- Sprinkle some grated cheese on top, dot with butter and brown in a fairly hot oven.

ŒUFS BROUILLÉS AUX MOULES

This Flemish entrée also makes a good luncheon dish

1 l. mussels (750 g.)
1 bouquet garni*
1 dl. water
60 g. butter
1 tbsp. brandy
6 eggs

3 tbsp. single cream
1 tbsp. chopped parsley
1 dtsp. chopped chervil
1 dtsp. chopped chives
1/2 dtsp. chopped tarragon leaves

- Scrape and clean the mussels, removing the beards and discarding any broken or open ones, and wash them under running water several times.
- Put the mussels in a deep, wide pan with 1 dl. water, salt, pepper, and the bouquet garni. Cover and cook over brisk heat until all the mussels have opened.
- Remove the mussels and shell them, reserving the flesh. Melt 30 g. of butter in a frying pan and sauté the mussels in it for 2-3 minutes, then flambé with the brandy and keep warm (but take care not to cook them further).
- Break the eggs in a bowl with the cream, salt and pepper to taste and whisk them lightly with a fork.
- Melt the remaining butter in a pan, pour in the eggs and stir with a wooden spoon over gentle heat until the eggs are set but still soft.
- Fold in the mussels and the chopped herbs and serve piping hot.

Fisherman's cottage in Flanders

Country café in the Meuse region, overleaf

OMELETTE À L'ARDENNAISE

One of the great standbys of Belgian cuisine

2 large slices Ardennes ham   4 eggs
    (or any uncooked cured ham)   salt, pepper
30 g. butter

- Chop the ham into bite-sized pieces and sauté them gently in butter for 3-4 minutes.
- Beat the eggs lightly, season generously with pepper but very moderately with salt.
- Add the beaten eggs to the frying pan over a brisk flame, shaking the pan to ensure that the omelette is evenly cooked. Make sure you do not overcook it. Fold the omelette in three with the fork, and slip it out on a warmed dish.

OMELETTE AUX HARENGS

A dish from Brussels — a creamy smoked herring omelette

4 smoked herring fillets   4 eggs
1.5 dl. milk   salt, pepper
30 g. butter   1 tbsp. chopped chives
2 tbsp. white wine   60 g. butter
2 tbsp. béchamel sauce (see p. 184)

- Place the herring fillets in a shallow dish, pour the milk over them and let them stand for 1 hour.
- Drain the fillets and pat them dry in a towel, then sauté them gently in 1 tbsp. butter.
- Cut them into 1-inch squares in the frying pan and when lightly golden, add the wine, let it bubble for 30 seconds and fold in the béchamel. Keep warm.
- Break the eggs into a bowl and whisk them gently with a fork, adding the salt, pepper and chives.
- Melt 2 tbsp. butter in an omelette pan, pour in the eggs, shaking the pan to ensure that the omelette is evenly cooked all over. Place the herring mixture in the middle, fold the omelette once and turn it upside down onto a warmed dish.

ŒUFS À LA CHIMACIENNE

A dish from Chimay, in the province of Hainaut : hardboiled eggs, stuffed with mushrooms and baked on a bed of creamed spinach

4 eggs
100 g. mushroom caps
1 shallot
1 tbsp. chopped parsley
75 g. butter

1 tsp. meat extract (e.g. Oxo etc.)
salt, pepper
500 g. spinach
0.5 dl. cream
50 g. breadcrumbs

- Hardboil the eggs for 10 minutes, then shell them under cold water.
- Chop the mushroom caps very finely and also the shallot and parsley.
- Sauté the shallot in 25 g. butter until it becomes translucent, add the chopped mushrooms, cook for a further 3 minutes then add the parsley. Season the mixture with the meat extract and pepper.
- Cut each egg in half lengthwise, remove the yolks and mash them into the mushroom mixture. Fill each half egg white with some of it.
- Cook the spinach in salted boiling water for 7-10 minutes, turn it into a colander and press a plate down on top of it to remove all excess water. Allow it to cool a little, then chop it finely.
- Return the spinach to the pan with 30 g. butter and the cream and adjust the seasoning. Heat it through.
- Put the spinach in a shallow gratin dish, arrange the stuffed eggs on top, sprinkle with breadcrumbs, dot with the remaining butter and put in a hot oven to brown.

ŒUFS POCHÉS À LA LIMBOURGEOISE

Eggs poached in a rich red wine sauce — a counterpart of the famous Burgundian œufs en meurette

100 g. mushroom caps
125 g. butter
2 shallots
1 clove garlic
1 dtsp. flour
3/4 l. red wine
1 tbsp. red wine vinegar

1 bay leaf
sprig of thyme
salt, pepper
4 eggs
4 slices white bread
1 tbsp. brandy

- Slice the mushroom caps finely then sauté them in 30 g. butter until golden. Reserve.
- Chop the shallots and garlic and sauté them gently in a deep saucepan in another 30 g. butter until translucent.
- Sprinkle the shallots and garlic with the flour, mixing it in well with a wooden spatula, then allow the mixture to colour slightly over medium heat.
- Pour in the wine gradually, add the vinegar, bayleaf and thyme and season carefully.
- Bring the sauce to the boil and simmer very gently for 40 minutes, making sure that the bottom of the pan does not burn.
- Cut the crusts off the slices of bread and trim them into round shapes, then sauté them in the remaining butter until golden on both sides. Remove them to a serving dish and keep warm.
- Poach the eggs in the sauce for 3-4 minutes, then drain them very carefully and put each egg on a slice of fried bread.
- Strain the sauce, add the brandy, fold in the mushrooms and pour carefully over the eggs. Serve at once.

Grand Place, Brussels

ŒUFS POCHÉS À LA BRUXELLOISE

An egg dish in which the creamy sauce counteracts the slightly bitter taste of chicory

4 blind-baked tartlets
3 large chicons (chicory)
60 g. butter

3 tbsp. Béchamel sauce
4 eggs
4 tbsp. thick cream

- Warm up the blind-baked tartlets in the oven.
- Chop the chicons finely and simmer them in 60 g. butter until they are cooked but still firm *(al dente)*.
- Blend the chicons with the Béchamel sauce and garnish the blind-baked tartlets with this mixture.
- Poach the eggs in vinegared water and place one egg in each tartlet.
- Cover each egg with a spoonful of cream cream and serve at once.

ŒUFS POCHÉS GAMBRINUS

Eggs poached in beer, a Brussels dish

4 eggs
1/2 bottle Belgian beer (such as Kriek)
    or lager
60 g. butter
1 tbsp. flour

1/2 tsp. sugar
1 dl. cream
4 slices bread
1 tbsp. chopped parsley
salt, pepper

- Bring the beer to a boil in a saucepan.
- Break the eggs in small bowls and poach them in the beer for 3-4 minutes or until they are set.
- Remove the eggs with a slotted spoon, drain and keep warm.
- Strain the beer into a jug.
- Make a roux* with the butter and flour and add gradually the strained beer until the sauce is smooth and thick. Add the sugar and cream, and mix well. Adjust seasoning.
- Cut off the crusts of the slices of bread and trim them into ovals or rounds, then fry them in the remaining butter.
- Put one egg on each slice of fried bread, spoon the sauce over and sprinkle with chopped parsley.
- Serve very hot.

ŒUFS MOLLETS À L'ANVERSOISE

Eggs on a bed of buttered hopshoots — a speciality of Antwerp

4 eggs
250 g. hopshoots
water
salt, pepper

1 dtsp. vinegar
lemon juice
90 g. butter
4 slices white bread

- Wash the hopshoots and put them in a pan filled with salted, boiling water. Add a few drops of lemon juice. Cook the hopshoots for about 10 minutes. They should remain firm *(al dente)*.
- When they are done, drain them thoroughly and toss them in 30 g. butter. Check the seasoning and keep them warm in a warmed salad bowl.
- Boil the eggs for exactly 5 minutes in water to which you have added a dessertspoon of vinegar.
- Meanwhile cut the crusts off the slices of bread and trim them into oval shapes, then fry them quickly in the remaining butter until they are golden and crisp on both sides. Arrange the bread on top of the hopshoots.
- Place the eggs under running cold water and shell them with great care, since the yolk will still be runny. Place each egg on its corresponding slice of fried bread and serve warm.

ŒUFS BROUILLÉS À LA WALLONNE

A comforting luncheon dish of eggs with black and white boudin

6 eggs
2 pieces boudin blanc*,
    about 15 cm long
2 pieces boudin noir*,
    about 15 cm long

80 g. butter
1 apple
1 tbsp. single cream
salt, pepper

- Sauté the pieces of black and white boudins in 30 g. butter for 5-8 minutes on each side, then drain them on kitchen paper, cut them into rounds 2 cm. thick and keep warm.
- Break the eggs into a bowl and beat lightly with a fork, adding salt, pepper and a tablespoon of cream.
- Peel, quarter and core the apple and slice it thinly, then sauté the slices gently in 25 g. butter until they change colour. Keep warm.
- Melt the remaining butter in a saucepan, add the beaten eggs and stir with a wooden spoon over a low flame until the scrambled eggs are set but still soft.
- Arrange the eggs in the middle of the serving dish, with alternate slices of white and black boudins and apples all around them, and serve hot.

Women ironing ; photograph by Wilmotte, 1886

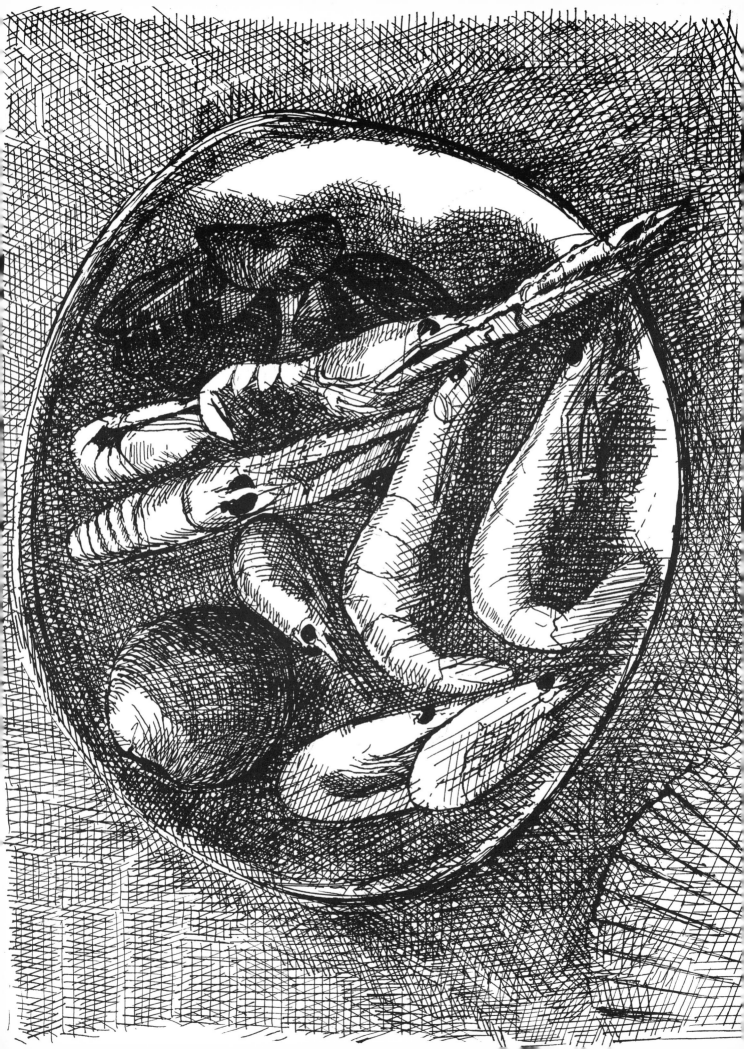

shellfish

HUÎTRES GRATINÉES

Baked oysters with shallot butter

4 doz. oysters　　　　　　　　**2 tbsp. minced parsley**
150 g. butter　　　　　　　　　**salt, pepper**
2 shallots　　　　　　　　　　　**breadcrumbs**

- Open the oysters carefully, reserving both shells and liquid. Strain the liquid into a saucepan and bring to the boil. Lift the flesh off the oysters with a small fork and poach in the liquid for 1 minute. Then drain and reserve.

- Preheat the oven to a high temperature.

- Mince the parsley and shallots very finely and work them into the butter until it is soft and creamy. Season with salt and pepper to taste.

- Put the poached oysters back in their shells, fill them up with the shallot butter, sprinkle with breadcrumbs and bake in the hot oven for 5 minutes. Serve very hot.

MOULES AU VIN BLANC

Similar to the French moules marinières but with the typically Belgian addition of celery

2 l. mussels (2.250 kg.)
2 onions
2 shallots
1 tbsp. chopped parsley
2 tbsp. chopped celery
2.5 dl. dry white wine

25 g. butter
freshly ground black pepper
1 lemon
1 egg yolk
1 tbsp. butter
1 tbsp. flour

- Scrape and clean the mussels thoroughly, removing the beards and discarding any broken or open ones. Wash them in several waters.
- Chop the onions, shallots, celery and parsley and put them in a deep saucepan with the butter, wine and freshly ground black pepper, but no salt.
- Bring the saucepan's contents to the boil and simmer gently for 5 minutes. Add the mussels, cover the pan and cook over medium heat, shaking the pan occasionally, until all the mussels have opened.
- While the mussels are cooking, prepare the beurre manié* by working together 1 tbsp. butter and 1 tbsp. flour in a bowl. Add the juice of 1 lemon and beat in the egg yolk.
- When the mussels have opened, drain them over a saucepan, reserving the liquid, and place them in a deep tureen.
- Place the saucepan with the liquid over gentle heat and add the beurre manié, whisking away all the time. Do not let it boil.
- Pour the sauce over the mussels and serve at once.

Fishing boats at Montgomery dock, Ostend

MOULES À LA BIÈRE

Mussels with beer, a Flemish speciality

2 l. mussels (2.250 kg)
2 onions
2 shallots
1 stick celery
1 tbsp. butter

33 cl. (1 bottle) pale ale
1 teaspoon cornflour
3 egg yolks
150 g. cream
salt, pepper

- Scrape and clean the mussels thoroughly, removing the beards and discarding any broken or open ones. Wash them in several waters.
- Chop the onions, shallots and celery finely.
- In a very deep saucepan, melt the butter.
- Add the mussels and stir.
- Pour in the beer, add the pepper and very little salt, cover the saucepan and cook the mussels over a medium flame until they have all opened.
- Remove the mussels, reserving the liquid.
- Open the mussels, leaving them on the half shell, and layer them in a wide, semi-shallow serving dish.
- Strain the liquid into a smaller saucepan.
- Mix the cornflour into a paste with a little water and add it to the liquid.
- Heat this to just under simmering point.
- Beat the egg yolks and cream and gradually beat in a little hot liquid.
- Pour this mixture into the saucepan, whisking all the time, until it thickens ; it must not boil.
- Check the seasoning and pour over the mussels.

MOULES DU NAVIGATEUR

Mussels with a hint of curry — a dish that recalls the exotic destinations of some of Antwerp's sailors

1 kg. mussels
1 large onion
1 stick celery
1 tbsp. chopped parsley
50 g. butter
2 dl. water

1 tsp. flour
1 tsp. curry powder
1 egg yolk
juice of 1/2 lemon
salt, pepper

RICE
1 tbsp. butter
long-grain rice

water
salt

- Scrape and clean the mussels thoroughly, removing the beards and discarding any broken or open ones. Wash them in several waters.
- Chop the onion, celery and parsley finely and put them in a deep saucepan with the water and 25 g. of butter.
- Bring to the boil, add the mussels, cover the pan and cook them over medium heat until they are all open.
- Strain the mussels over a saucepan and reserve the liquid.
- Meanwhile you will have cooked the rice : melt the butter in a saucepan, add the rice, stirring, then the water and salt. Bring to the boil, then cover, lower the heat and cook until tender but not mushy.
- In a saucepan, melt 25 g. butter, add the flour to make a roux*, then the curry powder, and pour in little by little enough of the mussel liquid to make a quarter of a litre. Whisk mixture all the time.
- Away from the heat, beat in the egg yolk and lemon juice, check the seasoning and put the mussels into the sauce.
- Heat through and serve in the centre of a dish filled with rice.

The fish market at Brussels, overleaf

COQUILLES SAINT-JACQUES EN WATERZOOI

Less classic than a lobster waterzooi, this is an delicious Flemish dish

8 large scallops (approx. 650-700 g.
    total weight out of shells)
1/4 l. fish stock (see p. 103)
1 carrot ⎫
1 onion ⎬   finely chopped
1 leek ⎭
1 stick celery

1 bouquet garni* (parsley, thyme,
    garlic, bayleaf)
1 glass dry white wine
1 dl. cream
2 eggs yolks
60 g. butter

- Melt the butter in a fairly large saucepan, and gently cook the finely chopped vegetables without colouring them for 5-10 minutes.
- Add the wine and simmer for 3 minutes.
- Next add the hot fish stock and bouquet garni and, with a lid on, simmer gently for 15 minutes.
- Meanwhile prepare the scallops : wash and dry them thoroughly and slice them thickly (approx. 3 to 4 slices per scallop).
- Poach the scallops for 8-10 minutes in the stock.
- Beat the egg yolks and cream thoroughly together.
- Remove the bouquet garni from the liquid.
- Check that the scallops are cooked (they should still have a bite to them and not be mushy).
- Away from the heat, stir in the egg and cream mixture and return the pan to a gentle heat, stirring until the liquid thickens slightly — be careful not to let it boil or your sauce will curdle.

Serve this as a starter with crusty bread for a special dinner party, but it may also be served as a supper or luncheon dish, followed by salad and cheese.

Serves 4-6 people as a starter depending on your guests — 3 for lunch or supper.

BROCHETTES DE COQUILLES SAINT-JACQUES

Scallops wrapped in bacon and grilled — a Flemish dish, flavoured with chervil, that also makes a good first course

16 scallops
1 dl. dry white wine
4 shallots
2 tbsp. chopped parsley
175 g. butter

16 extra thin slices of bacon
2 tbsp. wine vinegar
salt, pepper
1 tbsp. chopped chives
1 tbsp. chopped chervil

- Wash and dry the scallops thoroughly. Separate the coral from the body and slice each scallop in half. Leave the coral whole.
- Put the wine in a saucepan with a little salt and pepper, bring to the boil and poach the scallops in this for 5 minutes, then drain them and reserve the liquid.
- Chop two of the shallots finely and cook them gently in 30 g. butter without allowing them to change colour. Add the chopped parsley, remove from the heat and, with a pastry brush, coat the scallops with the mixture.
- Cut the bacon slices in half lengthwise and wrap the scallops and their coral in them, then thread them onto four skewers.
- Melt 50 g. butter, brush the bacon-wrapped scallops with this and put them under a medium grill for 15 minutes, basting them with more butter if necessary and turning them frequently.
- While the scallops are under the grill, prepare the sauce : chop the remaining shallots finely and put them in a pan with two tbsp. of the reserved poaching liquid and the vinegar. Bring to the boil and simmer until the liquid has reduced considerably.
- Away from the heat, beat in the remaining butter cut into small pieces, whisking until it is perfectly blended and the sauce is smooth. Add the herbs and pour the sauce in a warmed sauceboat.
- Serve the brochettes and sauce separately. The quantities given above serve four people as a main dish and six as a starter.

CRABES GRATINÉS

For this baked dish from Flanders, choose the large heavy crabs called tourteaux

4 large live crabs
2 carrots
1 onion
bouquet garni*
3-4 l. water
1 dl. wine vinegar
60 g. butter

150 g. mushroom caps
juice of 1/2 lemon
1 tbsp. flour
1/2 l. milk
1 tsp. French mustard
50 g. grated Swiss cheese
salt, pepper

- Scrape the carrots and cut them in rounds, chop the onion roughly and put them in a very large deep pan with 3-4 litres water, the vinegar and the bouquet garni. Bring to the boil and simmer for 15-20 minutes.
- Wash the crabs and throw them in the boiling water. Cook for 20 minutes then take them out, drain them and allow them to cool.
- Preheat the oven to a moderately hot temperature.
- Chop the mushrooms finely and sprinkle the lemon juice over them.
- Melt 30 g. butter in a saucepan and make a roux* with the flour, then add the milk, whisking all the time, to make a smooth béchamel (see p. 184). Season with salt and pepper and, away from the heat, add 1 teaspoon French mustard and 25 g. grated Swiss cheese.
- Remove the crabs' claws, break them with a nutcracker and remove all the meat. Also remove all the creamy, edible flesh from the shells. Chop up all the crab meat. Reserve the shells.
- Fold into the béchamel the chopped mushrooms and crab meat. Check the seasoning and fill the crab shells with the mixture.
- Sprinkle with the remaining grated cheese, cut up the rest of the butter into small pieces, dot the crab shells with it. Bake the crabs in a moderately hot oven until the top is gratinéed. Serve piping hot.

Bathing belles on the Belgian coast

HOMARD À LA GUEUZE

A delicious and unusual dish of lobster cooked in beer

2 live lobsters
1 onion
2 shallots
1 clove garlic
2 carrots
2 sticks celery

1/2 tsp. tarragon
35 g. butter
1/2 l. Gueuze (or a similar beer)
2 dl. single cream
2 egg yolks
salt, pepper

- Fill a very large saucepan with water, salt it, bring it to the boil and throw in the live lobsters for 2 minutes to kill them. Drain them and allow them to cool a little. (If you object to killing them yourself, you may buy freshly cooked lobsters from your fishmonger, but frozen lobsters are not really suitable for this subtle dish).

- Split each lobster in half lengthwise, keeping the shell halves intact. Remove the sand sacs in the heads and the intestinal tubes. Reserve the coral and green matter in a bowl. Remove the rest of the meat and chop it fairly roughly. Break the claws, remove the meat and chop it as well.

- Chop the onion, shallots, garlic, carrots, celery and tarragon finely.

- Melt 35 g. butter in a pan, put in the lobster meat and cook until it turns red, then add the vegetables. Cook for a further 2 minutes, then pour in the beer and simmer very gently with the lid on for 20 minutes.

- In the bowl containing the lobster coral and green matter, add the egg yolks and cream and blend well together.

- When the lobsters are done, strain the liquid into another saucepan, keeping the shellfish and vegetables warm. Boil the liquid rapidly to reduce it by about one third, then away from the heat stir in gradually the egg and cream mixture. Return the pan to a gentle heat, stirring with a wooden spoon until the sauce thickens. It must not boil.

- Add the lobster and vegetable mixture to the sauce, season well with salt and pepper, give it another stir then fill each lobster half-shell with it, and serve at once.

HOMARD GANDA

A classic lobster dish in the grand manner

2 lobsters, live or freshly cooked
    (see page 78)
2 slices cooked ham
100 g. mushroom caps
2 shallots
2 tbsp. brandy

2 dl. white wine
1 dl. port
salt, pepper
2 egg yolks
2 dl. single cream

- Prepare the lobsters as described in the first two paragraphs of page 79, but do not keep the shell halves.
- Chop the ham, shallots and mushrooms finely.
- Melt 35 g. butter in a large pan, put in the lobster meat and cook it for about 1 minute, then add the ham, shallots and mushrooms and continue to cook gently for another two minutes.
- Pour the warmed brandy into the pan and set it alight to flambé the shellfish and vegetables, then pour in the wine and port, season to taste, cover and cook gently for 20 minutes.
- Beat the egg yolks into the cream and add this to the reserved coral and green matter, then away from the heat beat it into the lobster mixture, making sure that it thickens without boiling.
- Check the seasoning and serve in a warm tureen with buttered noodles.

ÉCREVISSES À LA NAGE

An exquisitely delicate dish of crayfish in court-bouillon, from Liège

24 live crayfish

FOR THE COURT-BOUILLON

1 carrot
3 shallots
2 medium onions
1 celery heart
4 dl. dry white wine
2 dl. water
6 sprigs parsley

2 sprigs thyme
1 bayleaf
1/4 teasp. salt
6 black peppercorns
25 g. butter
1 tsp. chopped parsley

- First make the court-bouillon : slice the carrot into rounds, chop the onions, shallots and celery heart and put all of these into a large saucepan with the wine, water, parsley, thyme, bayleaf, peppercorns and salt.
  Bring to the boil and simmer for 20 minutes.

- Remove the intestinal gut from the crayfish by pulling it out with a small knife from under the central flange of the tail.

- Put all the crayfish in the court-bouillon, bring to the boil again and simmer for 15 minutes.

- Take the crayfish out, put them in a warmed soup tureen and boil the liquid briskly so that it reduces by half. Add 25 g. butter and the chopped parsley and pour over the crayfish.

This dish is also very good cold, in which case you must omit the final addition of butter.

Fisherman on the Semois

PUDDING AUX ÉCREVISSES

Adaptation of a seventeenth-century recipe from Luxembourg

30 live crayfish

FOR THE COURT-BOUILLON

1 carrot	**2 dl. water**
2 shallots	**1 bouquet garni**
2 onions	**1/4 tsp. salt**
2 dl. dry white wine	

200 g. fresh white breadcrumbs	**125 g. castor sugar**
3/4 l. milk	**pinch of cinnamon**
125 g. butter	**1 clove**
200 g. cooked white	**pinch of nutmeg**
chicken meat	**8 egg whites**
30 g. chopped almonds	

- First make the court-bouillon by simmering together all the ingredients for 20 minutes.
- Remove the intestinal gut from each crayfish by pulling it out with a small knife from under the central flange of the tail and cook the crayfish in the court-bouillon for 15 minutes.
- Soak the breadcrumbs in the milk.
- Remove all the flesh from the crayfish, mince it and reserve.
- Pound the crayfish shells and head in a mortar. Melt the butter in a saucepan and add the pounded shells, mixing well. Add the water and boil for 3 minutes.
- Put the mixture through a fine-meshed strainer over a bowl, pressing down on the ingredients with a wooden spoon, then chill the resulting liquid.
- When the butter in the liquid has set, melt the mixture over gentle heat for about 5 minutes so that the water evaporates. What you have left is proper crayfish butter.
- Preheat the oven.
- Mince the chicken meat finely and mix it with the minced crayfish flesh and the chopped almonds. Beat in the milk and breadcrumb mixture and the crayfish butter. Work well together, then add the sugar and spices and mix thoroughly.
- Beat the egg whites until stiff, then fold them into the crayfish mixture.
- Butter a large cake mould and fill it with the mixture. Put the mould in a baking tin filled with water and bake in a medium to slow oven for 1 - 1 1/2 hours or until the pudding is set and golden.

The Château of Walzin on the Meuse, Dinant

fish

TRUITE ARDENNAISE

Trout in breadcrumbs with a butter sauce

4 trout	2 shallots
2 eggs	1 tsp. fresh tarragon
150 g. breadcrumbs	1 tbsp. wine vinegar
1 glass dry white wine	flour
150 g. softened butter	salt, pepper

- Clean the trout and remove fins and gills. Dust the fish with seasoned flour.

- Beat together the eggs. Let the fish stand in the beaten egg for a few minutes. Roll the fish in the breadcrumbs and fry the fish in hot oil and butter in a frying pan for 10 to 15 minutes, or until the fish are cooked and crispy brown on both sides.

- While the fish are cooking, place the finely chopped shallots, the tarragon and wine vinegar, in another saucepan and cook over a high heat. Away from the heat add the softened butter a little at a time, stirring constantly, until you have a creamy sauce. Season carefully with salt and pepper.

- Serve the sauce separately in a sauceboat.

TRUITE AU VIN ROUGE

Trout simmered in red wine, from the Ardennes

4 trout
100 g. butter
3 shallots
100 g. mushrooms
2 tbsp. flour

juice of one lemon
1 tbsp. chopped parsley
3/4 l. red wine
salt, pepper

(You will need a casserole big enough to hold the fish side by side and deep enough to take the liquid, and which can be used on top of the stove.)

- Melt the butter and sauté the finely chopped shallots until they just begin to soften. Add the sliced mushrooms.
- Brown gently and add the flour. Mix well and, when the flour has been soaked up by the butter, add the wine. Bring slowly to the boil and simmer for 10 minutes.
- Clean and wipe the trout dry. Add to the wine, with salt and pepper, and cook very, very gently so that the liquid is just simmering for 15 minutes.
- Place the trout on a warmed serving dish and reduce the sauce to thicken slightly. Check the seasoning.
- Away from the heat, add the lemon juice and stir in a walnut-sized piece of butter. Sprinkle with parsley and serve with boiled potatoes.

The Quai Vert, Bruges, overleaf

TRUITE À LA BIÈRE

Trout gently simmered in beer, from Liège

4 trout   100 g. cream
1 bottle of Abbey beer   sprig of thyme
3 shallots   1 bay leaf
200 g. mushrooms   salt, pepper

- Clean the trout and place in a shallow dish into which the fish fit snugly without over-lapping. Add the beer, thyme and bay leaf and marinate for 2 1/2 hours.
- Finely chop the shallots and thinly slice the mushrooms. Gently cook the shallots and mushrooms in a large covered frying pan for 10 to 15 minutes.
- Add the trout and marinade to the large frying pan, removing the bay leaf and thyme. Gently cook for 15 minutes or until the fish are cooked. Remove fish to a warmed serving dish.
- Add the cream to the sauce and reduce the sauce to half its original quantity. Season to taste.
- Pour the sauce over the trout and serve with boiled potatoes.

MAQUEREAUX À LA FLAMANDE

Mackerel baked on a bed of onions

4 mackerel
2 lemons
3 large onions
100 g. butter
1/2 glass wine vinegar
salt, pepper
30 g. butter

1 tbsp. chives
1 tbsp. parsley
1 tbsp. chervil
1 tsp. tarragon
1 shallot
2 cloves garlic
60 g. melted butter

- Clean the mackerel, remove heads and fins and stuff with the mixed fresh herbs and finely chopped garlic and shallot.
- Finely chop the onions and sauté in 30 g. of butter for 5 minutes, without browning.
- Butter an ovenproof dish into which the fish will snugly fit. Cover the bottom of the dish with the onions and lay the fish on top. Season with pepper.
- Cover the fish with the lemons cut into rounds. Sprinkle with the wine vinegar and melted butter. Cook in a hot oven for 15 to 20 minutes or until the fish is cooked.
- Serve with baked potatoes filled with sour cream and chives.

BLANQUETTE À L'OSTENDAISE

A delicious delicate stew of different kinds of fish, mussels and shrimps in a cream sauce

2 kg. small mixed fish (whiting, cod,
    haddock, red mullet, eel)
100 g. peeled prawns
1 l. mussels
2 l. court-bouillon (see p. 182)
75 g. butter

75 g. flour
2 egg yolks
0.5 dl. cream
juice of 1/2 to 1 lemon
1 tbsp. chopped parsley

- Scrub the mussels, remove the beards and wash them thoroughly 2 or 3 times.
- Make the court-bouillon (see p. 182).
- While the court-bouillon is simmering, prepare the fish. Clean it, remove all heads and fins and cut each fish into 2-inch pieces. Reserve the prawns.
- Put the cleaned mussels into the court-bouillon, bring to the boil and cook over medium heat for 5 minutes or until all shells have opened.
- Strain the liquid into a bowl. Remove the mussels and allow them to cool. Pour the liquid back into the saucepan once more and simmer very gently for 10 minutes. Remove the mussels from their shells. Just before the 10 minutes are up, add the prawns and mussels to heat them through. Strain the fish broth into a bowl, arrange the fish and shellfish in a deep serving dish and keep warm.
- Beat the egg yolks and cream thoroughly together.
- Make a roux* with the butter and flour and pour in the fish broth in a gentle but steady stream, whisking all the time with a wire whisk to avoid lumps. Let the sauce thicken without bringing it to the boil.
- Remove from the heat. Beat a spoonful of warm sauce into the egg yolk and cream mixture and very gradually add the rest to the sauce, taking care that it does not curdle. Add the lemon juice to taste. Adjust seasoning, adding salt and freshly-ground black pepper if necessary.
- Coat the fish and shellfish with some of the sauce and sprinkle with chopped parsley. Serve the rest of the sauce separately.

This blanquette may be served with steamed new potatoes or buttered noodles.

Flemish fisherman

LOTTE AUX POIREAUX

An unusual combination of monkfish and leeks, from Knokke

4 portions of monkfish	**2 tbsp. oil**
125 g. butter	**1 kg. leeks**
1.5 dl. cream	**salt, pepper**

- Clean and slice the leeks, removing any tough outer leaves. The pieces should be about 2 in. long. Sprinkle with salt.
- Gently cook the leeks in 30 g. of butter and 2 tbsp. of peanut oil. Cook with the lid on until soft, about 15 to 20 minutes.
- In the meantime, sauté the seasoned fish in 50 g. of butter so that it is golden brown on both sides and cooked right through (7 to 10 minutes for each side depending on the thickness of the fish portions).
- Remove the fish to a warmed serving dish. Drain the leeks, reserving their juices. Arrange the leeks around the fish.
- Melt the rest of the butter in the pan in which the fish was cooked. Add the liquid from the leeks and, stirring constantly, add the cream. Season with salt and pepper to taste and pour over the fish and leeks.

Serve with boiled potatoes.

SOLE OSTENDAISE

Sole with mussels and shrimps in a cream and egg yolk sauce

4 small sole
2 lemons
20 cooked mussels
200 g. shelled shrimps
1 glass dry white wine
sprig of thyme

bay leaf
60 g. butter
70 g. flour
2 egg yolks
salt, pepper

- Place the cleaned sole in a buttered ovenproof dish. A roasting tin will do if you don't have anything else big enough. Cover with wine, the juice of 1 1/2 lemons, bayleaf and the sprig of thyme. Cover with buttered silverfoil and cook in a hot oven for 20 to 30 minutes or until the fish are cooked. The exact time depends on your oven and the size of the fish.

- While the fish are cooking, melt 60 g. of butter in a saucepan and add the flour to make a roux*. Cook gently for 5 to 6 minutes.

- When the fish are cooked, place in a warmed serving dish. Add the fish juices to the roux and, stirring constantly, bring slowly to the boil.

- Away from the heat, incorporate gently the beaten egg yolks. Add the mussels and shrimps, check seasoning, add the rest of the lemon juice if the flavour needs sharpening.

- Return the saucepan to the heat and allow the shrimps and mussels to heat through thoroughly without bringing the sauce to the boil. This should take no more than a few minutes.

- Pour the sauce over the fish and serve with boiled potatoes.

TURBOT AUX CHICONS

Turbot on a bed of chicory in a cream sauce, from Brussels

4 portions of turbot
75 g. butter
1.5 dl. cream

1 tbsp. peanut oil
1 kg. small chicons (chicory)
salt, pepper

- Clean the chicons by thoroughly wiping them. Remove any brown outer leaves.
- Heat 30 g. of butter and the oil and sauté the chicons, season and cover the saucepan. Gently cook over a low heat for 1 hour.
- The fish will take about 10 to 15 minutes to cook, depending on the thickness of the portions, so organise your cooking accordingly.
- Melt the rest of the butter in a frying pan and brown the fish on both sides. Lower the heat and gently continue the cooking until the fish is cooked.
- Place the fish on a warmed serving dish. Surround with the well-drained chicons.
- Add cream to the pan in which the fish were cooked, scraping the bottom of the pan to make sure that you include all the goodness from the fish, season with salt and pepper and pour over the fish.

BEIGNETS DE POISSONS

Fish balls in batter, from Brussels

350 g. leftover fish, boned and skinned
500 g. boiled floury potatoes
1 clove garlic
2 tbsp. chopped parsley
1 tbsp. chopped chervil
1 tbsp. chopped chives
50 g. softened butter
2 egg yolks

BATTER

100 g. plain flour
tbsp. olive oil
1.5 dl lukewarm beer
whites of 2 eggs
pinch of salt

FOR THE BATTER :

- Mix the flour and salt with the oil and the beer, beating well together. Cover and leave in the kitchen, not the refrigerator or cold larder, until required. This gives the flour a chance to ferment slightly, which improves the texture of the batter. Just before the batter is required, beat the egg whites until stiff and fold in carefully.

- Remove the skin and any bones from the cooked fish. Mash the boiled potatoes and mix the fish, potatoes, chopped garlic, herbs and the softened butter together. Add the egg yolks one at a time ; the mixture should hold its own shape and be neither too dry nor too liquid. Use only one egg yolk if this gives the right consistency, or the second egg yolk and a drop of milk if the mixture is too dry.

- Season to taste.

- Take a tablespoon of the mixture ; roll between the palms of your hands, which you have floured, into a small ball ; continue until all the mixture has been used, renewing the flour on your hands from time to time.

- Using a fork, dip each ball in the batter and plunge into hot fat.

- When brown and crispy, remove and serve with tomato sauce or mayonnaise.

Rough weather at Ostend

POISSONS EN ESCAVÈCHE

A freshwater fish terrine, from Namur

1 kg. small freshwater fish
4 tbsp. butter
5 tbsp. flour
5 medium onions, sliced
4 gherkins, sliced
1 tbsp. gelatin

3 lemons, washed and sliced
1/4 l. tarragon wine vinegar
2 dl. water
1 tbsp. fresh tarragon, chopped
4 peppercorns
salt, pepper

- Clean the fish and dry thorougly. Dust them with seasoned flour. Melt the butter in a frying pan and cook the fish, for about 3 to 4 minutes on either side, or until cooked.

- Remove the fish from the pan and leave them to cool.

- Put the vinegar, water, finely chopped tarragon, crushed peppercorns and a pinch of salt into a saucepan and slowly bring to the boil. Sprinkle the gelatin into the saucepan and stir until it has melted.

- In a terrine that will hold the fish, onions and lemons snugly, arrange alternative layers of fish, sliced onion lemon rings, and slices of gherkin, finishing with a layer of lemon rings.

- Pour the gelatin liquid over the fish so that all the fish is completely covered.

- Leave in the refrigerator for 2 to 3 days before eating.

Serve with slices of thinly-cut brown bread.

The Our Valley, Vianden

ANGUILLES AU VERT

A classic Belgian dish of eels in herb sauce

1 kg. eels
125 g. butter
125 g. sorrel
50 g. parsley
100 g. chervil
6 sage leaves

6 leaves of lemon-flavoured verbena
2 shallots
2 glasses dry white wine
2 egg yolks
juice of 1 lemon
salt, pepper

- Clean the eels and cut into 2-inch pieces.
- Sauté the eel pieces and chopped shallots gently in the butter until they begin to brown. Add the finely chopped sorrel, parsley, chervil, sage, lemon verbena, the white wine and enough water to just cover the fish. Season with salt and pepper and simmer gently for 15 minutes or until the eel is cooked.
- Mix the egg yolks and lemon juice together, add 4 tbsp. of the sauce from the pan to the egg mixture. Away from the heat add the egg mixture to the sauce, mix well.
- Serve the eels either hot or cold.

The Church of St Gudule, Brussels

FILETS DE PLIE BLANKENBERGEOISE

Fillets of plaice with shrimps in a cream sauce

16 fillets of plaice
250 g. shrimps in shells
1 dl. fresh cream
1 small carrot ⎞
1 shallot ⎟
1 small leek ⎬ finely chopped
1 stick celery ⎠
1 tsp. tomato purée
1 tbsp. fresh tarragon
30 g. butter
small glass white wine
4 tbsp. brandy

cayenne pepper
salt, pepper

STOCK
1 small onion
1 leek
1 stick celery
1 carrot
1/2 l. water
bouquet garni (bay leaf, 3 parsley
        stalks, lemon rind)

- *First prepare the fish stock* : shell and remove heads from shrimps, reserving flesh for later. Roughly chop the vegetables for stock. Add vegetables, shells, heads, bouquet garni to water, season with pepper, no salt at this stage as the shells and heads may be salty enough. Simmer for 40 minutes and strain.

- In the butter, sauté the finely chopped vegetables for 3 to 4 minutes, add brandy and flambé. As the flames die down, add the white wine and two glasses of the prepared stock, the tarragon and tomato purée. Simmer gently for 15 minutes.

- Gently add the cream, stirring constantly. Add the shrimps and 2 pinches of cayenne pepper. Check seasoning.

- While you are preparing the sauce, cook the fillets in a frying pan a few at a time and keep warm until the sauce is ready.

- Arrange the fish on a serving dish and cover with the sauce. Serve with boiled potatoes.

Two views of Blankenberg

Farm at Annevoie in the Meuse Valley, overleaf

poultry and rabbit

FRICASSÉE DE POULET À LA MALINOISE

A delicate dish of chicken with cream and asparagus tips, from Mechelen

1 chicken
30 g. butter
1 tbsp. peanut oil
12 small onions
salt, pepper

1 kg. asparagus
2.5 dl. cream
2 egg yolks
juice of 1 lemon

- Cut the chicken into 8 pieces and sauté these quickly in a mixture of butter and oil until they are golden, then remove them into a casserole dish.

- In the same fat brown the baby onions and add them to the chicken. Season with salt and pepper and cook over very gentle heat for 45-50 minutes or until the chicken is cooked.

- In the meantime cut all the asparagus tips (about 3 inches long) and steam them over a pan of boiling water.

- When the chicken is done, remove it from the casserole and keep warm on a serving dish.

- Whisk the cream and egg yolks together, beat in a spoonful of the hot chicken juice, then pour in the cream mixture. Do not boil or it will curdle. Add the lemon juice, check the seasoning, fold in the asparagus tips to warm them through, then pour over the chicken.

- Serve with boiled new potatoes.

WATERZOOI GANTOIS

No Belgian cookbook would be complete without this famous classic from Ghent, a chicken and cream dish that is halfway between a soup and a stew

1 large chicken	1-1.5 l. strong-flavoured
2 onions	veal or chicken stock
2 shallots	4 egg yolks
3 leeks	1 dl. cream
3 sticks celery	juice of 1/2 - 1 lemon
3 carrots	1 tbsp. chopped parsley
4 parsley roots	salt, white pepper
60 g. butter	

- First chop all the vegetables finely and stew them gently in a large saucepan with 30 g. butter for 20 minutes (it is important to go through the bother of obtaining parsley roots for they give a flavour and texture which are quite unobtainable otherwise).
- Cut the chicken into 8 pieces and lay these on top of the vegetables.
- Pour enough veal or chicken stock (it must be well-flavoured and strong otherwise the entire dish will be spoilt) to cover. Season to taste with salt and freshly ground white pepper. Cover, bring to the boil and simmer very gently until the chicken pieces are cooked.
- While the chicken is cooking beat the egg yolks and cream together. Add the remaining 30 g. of butter and blend this in.
- Remove the chicken pieces to a warmed soup tureen and keep warm.
- Remove the parsley roots and sieve or mash them into the egg and cream mixture.
- Beat a spoonful of the hot liquid into the mixture then add it gradually to the soup, whisking all the time over a very gentle heat. Make sure it does not curdle. Season to taste with lemon juice, add the chopped parsley and pour over the chicken pieces in the soup tureen.
- Serve the waterzooi with boiled potatoes or toasted and buttered French bread.

Waterzooi is the subject of much discussion and controversy for there are as many recipes for it as there are families in Belgium. The recipe we have given here is for a classic chicken waterzooi but it may also be applied to rabbit.

CANARD DU MAÎTRE VERRIER

Roast ducklings stuffed with herbs

2 ducklings (with their livers)
50 g. pork fat
2 shallots ⎫
1 clove garlic ⎬ diced or chopped
6 mushrooms ⎬
1 truffle ⎭
1 tbsp. chopped sorrel

1 dstp. chopped tarragon
1 dstp. chopped chervil
1 dstp. chopped chives
pinch quatre épices
(powdered, cloves, nutmeg,
cinnamon, cayenne pepper)

FOR THE SAUCE

3 shallots
2 cloves garlic
juice of 1 orange

salt, pepper
beurre manié*
2 tbsp. Grand Marnier

100 g. butter
50 g. breadcrumbs
salt, pepper

- Remove the livers from the ducklings, chop them finely and add them to the diced pork fat, and chopped shallots, garlic, mushrooms, truffle and herbs. Season with salt, pepper and quatre épices, mix with 25 g. melted butter and stuff the ducklings with this.

- Brush the birds with another 25 g. melted butter, season with salt and pepper and put them in a medium to hot oven.

- When the ducklings are half-roasted take them out, brush their entire surface with a mixture of breadcrumbs and 50 g. melted butter and put them back in the oven to brown.

- When they are cooked, remove them and keep them warm while you prepare the sauce.

- Deglaze the pan juices by scraping and boiling them in a saucepan with a couple of tablespoons of Grand Marnier until the liquid is reduced by a third.

- Chop 3 shallots and 2 cloves of garlic and add them to the sauce with the juice of an orange.

- Thicken the sauce with beurre manié* and pour it over the ducklings.

Serve this dish with crisp green beans or a fricassée of spring vegetables (see recipe, p. 167).

Galeries St-Hubert, Brussels

CANARD BRAISÉ AUX NAVETS

A Namur cousin of the famous French dish

1 duck	12 small onions
60 g. butter	1 bouquet garni*
2 tbsp. peanut oil	2 tbsp. water
2 shallots } chopped	1 kg. new turnips
1 clove garlic }	2 tbsp. sugar

- Cut the duck in 8 pieces and brown these in a frying-pan in a mixture of 30 g. of butter and 2 tbsp. of oil, then remove them to a cast-iron casserole.

- Pour off excess fat and in the remaining juices sauté the chopped shallots and garlic and the small onions.

- When the vegetables change colour, add them to the duck in the casserole. Put in the bouquet garni and 2 tbsp. water, and season with salt and pepper. Bring to the boil, then turn the heat down, cover and simmer gently for half an hour.

- Meanwhile peel and trim the baby turnips and blanch them for 5 minutes in salted boiling water.

- Drain the turnips and sauté them in the remaining butter, with 2 tbsp. sugar, over a highish flame until they are golden and slightly caramelised, then add them to the duck and continue to cook until both duck and turnips are cooked.

- Check the seasoning and serve very hot in the casserole in which the duck has cooked.

PINTADE AUX CHICONS À L'ARDENNAISE

Guinea-fowl and Ardennes ham on a bed of chicory

1 guinea-fowl
4 slices Ardennes ham
2 onions
1 kg. chicons (chicory)
75 g. butter

3 tbsp. strong veal stock (see p. 183)
1 bouquet garni*
1 small glass madeira
salt, pepper

- Chop 2 slices of Ardennes ham in 1-inch pieces ; chop the onions finely. Clean and trim the chicons and remove any brown outer leaves.

- In a large saucepan or casserole sauté the ham and onions in 30 g. butter until they change colour, add the chicons, cover the pan and stew over low heat for 15 minutes.

- Meanwhile bard* the guinea-fowl with the remaining slices of ham and brown it quickly in another 30 g. butter.

- Place the guinea-fowl on top of the vegetables and ham, season to taste with salt and pepper, add the bouquet garni and moisten with the veal stock. Cook gently, un-covered, for about 50 minutes or until the bird is tender, then remove the guinea-fowl and vegetables to a serving dish and keep warm.

- Mix a walnut-sized piece of butter in the sauce, add the madeira, check the seasoning and pour into a sauceboat.

- Serve the bird and its sauce separately.

PINTADE AU CHOU ROUGE

A fragrant dish from Hainaut : guinea-fowl on a bed of red cabbage

1 guinea-fowl
1 red cabbage
150 g. smoked streaky bacon
    in one piece
50 g. butter
2 medium-sized onions
2 shallots

50 g. raisins
1 glass dry white wine
6 juniper berries, crushed
salt, pepper
1 sprig thyme
1 tbsp. white wine vinegar

- Slice the red cabbage finely. Dice the streaky bacon. Chop the onions and shallots.
- Sauté the bacon in half the butter. When it turns colour, add the onions, shallots, and raisins and continue to sauté gently for 3 minutes.
- Remove these to an earthenware or cast-iron ovenproof dish.
- Add the rest of the butter to the frying-pan and quickly brown the guinea-fowl on all sides.
- Remove the guinea-fowl and place it on the bed of vegetables in the ovenproof dish.
- Deglaze the pan juices with the white wine, bring to the boil rapidly and add it to the guinea-fowl.
- Place the sliced red cabbage all around it, season well with salt and pepper and the crushed juniper berries and bury the sprig of thyme in the cabbage.
- Cover the dish and cook in a medium oven for 1 to 1 1/2 hours.
- Just before serving, add the vinegar and mix well.

OIE À LA MOUTARDE

Roast goose in a mustard sauce, an eighteenth-century recipe from the Ardennes

FOR 6-8 people

1 young goose (with its liver)
2 shallots
2 onions
1 clove garlic
1/2 tbsp. dry thyme
1 tbsp. chopped parsley
1 tbsp. chopped chives

1 bay leaf
60 g. butter
salt, pepper
2 tbsp. French mustard
0.5 dl. white wine
1 tbsp. flour
1 tbsp. wine vinegar

- Remove the goose liver and chop it finely. Mix it in a bowl with the chopped shallots, onion, garlic and herbs, add 30 g. melted butter, salt and pepper and stuff the goose with this aromatic mixture.
- Roast the goose on a rack in the usual manner and gather its roasting juices in a pan below the rack. Use these to baste the bird often until it takes on a uniformly golden colour.
- When the goose is about three-quarters done, add a tbsp. of mustard to the pan juices, mix it in well and continue to baste the bird with it.
- When the goose is done, remove it and keep warm in a serving dish.
- Pour the pan juices into a saucepan and boil rapidly with the wine, skimming away most of the fat.
- In another saucepan make a roux* with 30 g. butter and 1 tbsp. flour, add the deglazed juices, the vinegar and another tbsp. mustard. Adjust the seasoning and pour over the bird.

View of Visé

OIE À L'INSTAR DE VISÉ

One of the most famous dishes of Belgium : goose, first boiled, then fried, served in a garlic-flavoured sauce

FOR 6-8 PEOPLE

1 goose
2 l. strong-flavoured veal stock
   (see p. 183)
3 onions
3 carrots
1 head of celery } roughly chopped
1 head of garlic
1 bouquet garni*
60 g. butter

2 tbsp. flour
10 cloves garlic
nutmeg
salt, pepper
4-6 tbsp. goose fat
4 egg yolks
1 dl. cream

- In order to minimise the scum that forms when you boil meat or fowl, use the following method (which is also applicable to veal blanquette and other similar dishes) : place the goose in a very large pan of cold water and bring it to the boil. Scum will form. Drain the goose at once and wash it free of scum in cold water. You can then proceed with the recipe.

- Put the goose back in the washed pan. Add the roughly chopped vegetables and the bouquet garni. Pour in the veal stock and enough water to cover the goose. Bring to the boil and cook over low heat for about 2 hours, or until the goose is cooked.

- Remove the goose from the pan, let it cool a little, then cut it into portions.

- In another saucepan, make a roux* with the butter and flour and pour in gradually 4 dl. of the strained cooking liquid, whisking until the sauce is smooth and thick.

- Crush the 10 cloves of garlic and add them to the sauce, together with a large pinch of nutmeg. Check the seasoning and keep warm.

- Melt the goose fat in a large frying-pan and when it is sizzling, sauté the goose portions in it until they are golden all over. Arrange them on a serving dish and keep warm.

- Whisk the egg yolks and cream together, beat in gradually a couple of tablespoons of the hot sauce, then add the mixture to the sauce in the pan and reheat gently, without boiling or it will curdle.

- Pour some of the sauce over the goose and put the rest in a sauceboat.

- Serve with roast potatoes or roustiquettes à la graisse d'oie (see recipe, p. 166).

LAPIN AUX CERISES À LA TOURNAISIENNE

A fricassée of rabbit with cherries

1 rabbit
30 g. butter
12 small onions
1 tbsp. flour
2 tbsp. brandy
3 dl. dry white wine

1 bouquet garni*
1 tbsp. brown sugar
salt, pepper
300 g. sour cherries
1 tbsp. chopped parsley

- Cut the rabbit in 8 pieces and brown these quickly in 30 g. butter in a thick-bottomed or cast-iron casserole.

- Add the small onions and continue to cook until these have taken on colour.

- Sprinkle the rabbit and onions with flour and stir it with a wooden spoon, then pour in the brandy and flambé. Add the white wine, the bouquet garni, the brown sugar ; check the seasoning. Bring to the boil and, turning the heat down, simmer until the rabbit is cooked.

- Ten minutes before the rabbit is done, add the cherries (without their stones if you can be bothered to remove them without bruising the fruit).

- Just before serving, sprinkle the parsley over the rabbit and serve with croûtons of bread fried in butter.

LAPIN À LA GUEUZE

A rabbit stew with prunes and sultanas

1 rabbit
1 large onion
1 carrot
125 g. diced bacon
1 l. Gueuze (or similar beer)
60 g. butter
12 small onions
200 g. prunes (soaked for 1/2 hour
    before use)

100 g. sultanas
1 sprig thyme
1 bay leaf
3 cloves
1 clove garlic
2 tbsp. redcurrant jelly
1 tbsp. wine vinegar
2 tbsp. flour
salt, pepper

- Cut the rabbit into regular-sized pieces, about 8 in all. Place in a marinade made from the chopped onion and carrot, 1 litre of beer, thyme, bay leaf, cloves, crushed garlic, salt and pepper. Marinate for at least 12 hours.

- Drain and dry the rabbit. Melt the butter in a casserole, cook the diced bacon until the fat is running, remove with a slotted spoon and in its place sauté the rabbit pieces until brown. Stir in the flour.

- Add the marinade ; the liquid should just cover the rabbit. Add more beer if necessary. Bring to the boil.

- Add the bacon, redcurrant jelly, onions, sultanas and prunes. Cover and simmer for 1 hour.

- Remove the rabbit to a warmed serving dish ; reduce the sauce by a third, by boiling quickly without a lid. Stir in a walnut-sized lump of butter and pour over the rabbit.

Serve with plain boiled potatoes.

A cobbled street in Liège, overleaf

LAPIN AU CHOU

A delicious spring dish of rabbit with new cabbage

1 rabbit
2 new green cabbages
200 g. streaky bacon in one piece
3 onions
2 carrots

30 g. butter
1 dl. water
6 crushed juniper berries
salt, pepper

- Dice the bacon, chop the onions and carrots, cut the rabbit in 8 pieces.
- Cut each new green cabbage into quarters and blanch them for 3 minutes in boiling salted water, then drain them.
- Sauté the rabbit pieces in butter in a frying-pan and, when they are golden, remove then to a cast-iron or heavy-bottomed casserole.
- In the same fat, sauté the diced bacon, carrots and onions until they change colour.
- Arrange the cabbage among the pieces of rabbit. Season well with salt and pepper.
- Add the bacon, onions, carrots, crushed juniper berries, and 1 dl. water, cover and cook gently until the rabbit is quite tender.

Above : Market day at Louvain
Below : Restaurant at Rochefort

meat

QUEUE DE BŒUF EN HOCHEPOT

Casserole of oxtail and pig's trotters, from Flanders

1 oxtail	6 carrots
2 pig's trotters	6 turnips
1 small cabbage	salt, pepper
4 onions	1 tbsp. lard or dripping
1 kg. potatoes	

- Cut the oxtail into 2-inch pieces and the pig's feet into 4. Place in a large saucepan, cover with cold water, season, bring to the boil and simmer for 1 1/2 hours, skimming frequently.

- Roughly chop the onions, carrots and turnips and add to the saucepan. Remove any tough outer leaves and the centre stalk from the cabbage and roughly chop. Add to the saucepan and cook for a further hour.

- Peel and quarter the potatoes, add to the casserole and simmer for a further 30 minutes. You may find that you have to add extra water before you add the potatoes.

- Season to taste and serve boiling hot.

CARBONNADES FLAMANDES

Beef stew simmered in beer, one of the great Belgian classics

1 kg. stewing steak
3 onions
1 carrot
1/3 l. beer
1/3 l. water
2 tbsp. brown sugar

1 tbsp. wine vinegar
thyme
bay leaf
salt, pepper
50 g. butter
flour

- Cut the meat into fairly large pieces, about 2-3 inches square. Dust with seasoned flour.
- Melt the butter in a heavy-bottomed casserole and sauté the beef. Add the chopped onions and finely chopped carrot and add to the beef ; brown lightly.
- Add the water and beer (the liquid should cover the meat so add more beer if necessary), the vinegar, salt and pepper, the bay leaf and sprig of thyme, bring to the boil and simmer over a low heat for 2 hours.
- Add the sugar and simmer for a further 15 minutes. Serve with boiled potatoes.

Rue du Rouleau, Bruges

OISEAUX SANS TÊTE

Beef parcels, filled with veal and pork stuffing and cooked in stock

4 large, thin slices of beef
      about 8 x 3 inches
350 g. veal and pork, minced
150 g. Ardennes ham, minced
2 eggs
1 onion
2 shallots
30 g. butter

1 clove garlic
1 tsp. chopped parsley
1/2 l. stock
1 bay leaf
sprig thyme
1 tsp. tomato purée
50 g. fresh breadcrumbs
salt, pepper

- Beat the beef slices as thin as possible.
- Make the stuffing by mixing together the veal and pork mince, ham, chopped shallots, finely chopped garlic, breadcrumbs, parsley, salt and pepper, and bind with the lightly beaten eggs.
- Divide the stuffing into 4 portions and put one on each slice of beef. Roll them up and tuck in ends to prevent the stuffing from escaping. Make a parcel by tying securely with kitchen string.
- In a shallow casserole melt the butter and sauté the beef parcels until light brown on both sides. Remove and keep to one side. Add the chopped onion and cook for 3-4 minutes. Return the beef parcels to the casserole, pour over the stock, add the tomato purée, bay leaf and sprig of thyme, season to taste, cover and cook in a medium hot oven for 1 hour.
- Remove the string, serve with the sauce and mashed potatoes.

Maison du Roi, Grand Place, Brussels

JARRET DE BŒUF EN CASSEROLE

Shin of beef cooked slowly in red wine, from Tournai

1.5 kg. shin of beef
100 g. piece of bacon, diced
2 cloves garlic
1/2 l. beef stock (see p. 183)
1 tbsp. olive oil
2 large onions

1/4 l. red wine
bunch of parsley
bay leaf
sprig thyme
salt, pepper

- In a heavy-bottomed casserole heat the olive oil and sauté the diced bacon until the fat begins to run. Add the sliced onions and cook for 2 more minutes.

- Remove the skin and excess fat from the shin of beef, cut lengthways into fairly thick pieces and place on top of the onions. Add the crushed garlic and the parsley, bay leaf and sprig of thyme and pour in the wine. Over a high heat bring to the boil, and boil for 2 or 3 minutes ; add the stock and bring to the boil again.

- Cover the casserole with foil and then the lid, transfer to the oven and cook slowly for 3 hours.

- Serve with boiled potatoes or rice.

JARRET DE VEAU PRINTANIER

Shin of veal with spring vegetables

1.5 kg. shin of veal
    cut into thick slices
50 g. butter
2 tbsp. peanut oil
24 small onions
6 new carrots, cut into
    rounds

8 new turnips, whole
8 new potatoes,
    whole or quartered
2 dl. dry white wine
1 bouquet garni*
salt, pepper
beurre manié*

- In a frying-pan, brown the slices of shin of veal in a mixture of butter and oil then arrange them in a deep, preferably cast-iron casserole, so that they remain upright to prevent marrow in the bone from falling out during the cooking.

- In the same frying-pan, sauté the small onions, carrots and potatoes for 2 minutes then add to the meat.

- Deglaze the pan juices by scraping them briskly over high heat after pouring in the white wine, then spoon over the meat and vegetables in the casserole.

- Add a bouquet garni, season with salt and pepper, bring to the boil, cover and cook very gently so that it is barely simmering, for 1 1/2 hours or until the veal is tender.

- If the sauce in the pan is too liquid after cooking, thicken it with a little beurre manié.

A watermill on the river Légia

FOIE DE VEAU À LA LIÉGEOISE

An unusual sweet-sour recipe for calf's liver

4 slices calf's liver
50 g. streaky bacon in one piece
50 g. butter
2 shallots, chopped
1 tbsp. red wine vinegar

1 tbsp. redcurrant jelly
50 g. sultanas, soaked in
    1 dl. red wine for 1 hour
beurre manié*
salt, pepper

- Dice the bacon and blanch it in boiling water for 2 minutes, then strain and reserve.

- Sauté the slices of liver in 50 g. butter over high heat so that they brown quickly on both sides, then turn the heat down and cook for another 3 minutes. Season them with salt and pepper and remove them to a hot serving dish. Keep them warm while you prepare the sauce.

- Sauté the bacon in the same pan, add the shallots and continue to cook until they take on colour.

- Add the sultanas in their marinade of red wine, the vinegar and redcurrant jelly and boil rapidly to evaporate the alcohol.

- Check the seasoning and thicken the sauce with a little beurre manié*, then pour it over the liver and serve with mashed potatoes.

The Montagne de Bueren, Liège

ROGNONS DE VEAU AU GENIÈVRE

Juniper berries, genever and beer give a distinctive flavour to this dish of veal kidneys, from Liège

4 veal kidneys
2 shallots
30 g. butter
2 tbsp. genever

2 dl. beer
8 crushed juniper berries
2 tbsp. cream
salt, pepper

- Remove the fat from the kidneys and cut them into 1-inch pieces. Chop the shallots, finely.
- Sauté the shallots in the butter until translucent, add the kidneys and cook them quickly in the butter. They must be brown on the outside but remain a little rosy inside.
- When the kidneys are done, remove them to a serving dish and keep warm.
- Pour away excess fat, add the genever and beer to the pan and scrape with a wooden spoon. Allow the liquid to boil down a little.
- Add the crushed juniper berries and season with salt and plenty of freshly ground black pepper. Continue to boil until the liquid is reduced by one third. Pour in the cream and spoon the sauce over the kidneys.

TERRINE DES POLDERS

A delicious summer dish of cold veal from the Antwerp region

500 g. boneless shoulder
    of veal
500 g. green bacon
    in one piece
3 onions
3 carrots   } roughly
3 leeks   } chopped
1 head celery
1 bunch parsley

2 sprigs thyme
1 bay leaf
6 peppercorns
1 1/2 l. good veal stock (see p. 183)
1 tbsp. tarragon vinegar
30 g. powdered gelatin
75 g. pickled button onions
75 g. gherkins
2 lemons, sliced and blanched

- Put the veal and bacon in a wide, deep saucepan with cold water to cover and bring to the boil. Remove at once, wash off the scum in cold water and wash the saucepan also.
- Put the veal and bacon back into the saucepan. Add the chopped vegetables, herbs and seasoning (do not add salt), pour in the veal stock and enough water to cover the meat. Bring to the boil and simmer over low heat until the meat is absolutely tender.
- Remove the veal and bacon and allow to cool.
- Strain the liquid into another saucepan, remove excess fat with a spoon or kitchen paper and boil down to about 1 l.
- Add 1 tbsp. vinegar and the gelatin, whisking so that it is completely dissolved. Check the seasoning but avoid salting too much.
- Slice the veal and bacon, pour a little liquid in the bottom of a terrine and line the bottom with slices. Fill the terrine with alternating layers of meat, pickled onions, sliced gherkins and thinly sliced blanched lemon rounds until the terrine is filled.
- Pour the liquid in and chill the terrine for at least 12 hours. You may serve this with potato salad or a crisp green salad.

*Ruins of the medieval château
at Laroche in the Ardennes*

Rue de la Station, Messancy, overleaf

NOIX DE PORC ARLONAISE

Boned loin of pork with prunes, from Arlon

1 kg. loin of pork
1 dl. white wine
2 dl. beef stock
pinch dried thyme
1 bay leaf
2 tbsp. oil
salt, pepper

FOR THE PRUNES

300 g. dried prunes
50 g. sugar
1/4 l. water
1/4 l. dry white wine

- Leave the prunes to soak for at least 3 hours in the white wine and water.

- In a small casserole brown the pork on all sides in the oil, spoon out any excess fat, add the dl. of white wine, cook over a high heat and let the wine evaporate. Pour the stock over the pork, season and add the thyme and bay leaf, cover and simmer on a very low heat for 2 hours.

- While the pork is cooking, simmer the prunes with the sugar and the liquid in which they have been soaked until they have swollen and there is very little liquid left in the saucepan.

- Add the prunes and their liquid to the pork after it has been simmering for 2 hours. Cook for a further 15 minutes.

- Slice the pork and place on warmed serving dish, surrounded with mashed potatoes.

CARRÉ DE PORC AUX QUETSCHES

Loin of pork with plums, from the Ardennes

1 loin pork (1.2 kg.)
750 g. dark purple plums
3 shallots
2 onions
4 cloves
100 g. butter

1 small glass eau-de-vie*
2 tbsp. redcurrant jelly
3 tbsp. cream
1/2 tbsp. flour } to make
1/2 tbsp. butter } beurre manié*
salt, pepper

- Season the pork with salt and pepper, stick the cloves into the fat of the pork. Melt 50 g. butter and brown the pork on all sides. Add the chopped onions and shallots, and cook for a further 5 minutes.

- Surround the pork with 250 g. of the plums, place in a hot oven and cook for 1 hr 15 minutes or until the meat is cooked.

- In 50 g. butter stew the rest of the plums and cook gently over low heat for 15-20 minutes. The plums should still look like plums and not be mushy.

- When the pork is cooked, remove to a warmed serving dish. Pour off excess fat from the roasting tin and strain the rest of the juices and plums through a sieve, pressing all the juice and goodness from the plums.

- Return to roasting tin, add the eau-de-vie and flambé. Add the redcurrant jelly and cream, cook gently for 2-3 minutes, add the beurre manié a bit at a time, check the seasoning.

- Arrange the cooked plums around the pork and serve the sauce separately.

HOCHEPOT DES FLANDRES

A comforting winter stew, from Flanders

4 pork chops
500 g. pork and veal sausages
1 small green cabbage
2 onions
3 sticks celery
5 leeks
4 turnips

4-5 carrots
1 kg. potatoes
sprig thyme,
bay leaf
2 cloves garlic
salt, pepper
30 g. butter

- In a large saucepan brown the chops and sausages for 4-5 minutes and reserve sausages.
- Add the chopped cabbage, onions, celery, leeks, turnips, carrots, and the crushed garlic, as well as the thyme, and bay leaf. Cover with cold water, season with salt and pepper, and simmer for 2 hours.
- Add the peeled and chopped potatoes, and the sausages and continue to cook for another 30 minutes.
- Serve with 2 or 3 different mustards.

CIVET DE PORC

A delicious casserole of pork in red wine, from Liège

1.2 kg. boned pork loin
2 onions
1 carrot
1 clove garlic
1 clove
2 dl. pig's blood
50 g. butter

sprig thyme
bay leaf
1 bt. red wine
20 small onions
250 g. mushrooms
2 tbsp. flour
salt, pepper

(The pig's blood is essential for this dish — it is what gives the sauce body and character. Most butchers will supply it on request.)

- Cut the meat into pieces about 2 inches square, marinate it for 24 hours, longer if possible, in the wine with the carrot and onion finely chopped, crushed clove and chopped clove of garlic, the sprig of thyme and bay leaf, salt and pepper.

- Drain the pork and dry on a tea towel, reserving the marinade. Melt the butter in a heavy-bottomed casserole, and sauté the meat until lightly brown all over. Add the mushrooms and small onions and sauté for a further 5 minutes ; sprinkle with the flour. When the flour has been absorbed by the fat in the pan, add the marinade ; the marinade should cover the meat — if it does not, add some water. Simmer over a low heat for 2 hours or until the meat is very tender.

- Add the pig's blood and continue to cook for a further 5 minutes, check seasoning and serve with boiled potatoes.

Tea at « Siska », Knokke-le-Zoute

SAUCISSE D'ARLON

A warming winter family dish of sausages, potatoes and turnips

400 g. pork sausage
500 g. turnips
500 g. potatoes
3 shallots
sprig thyme

1 bay leaf
2 tbsp. dry white wine or
    dry cider
50 g. butter
salt, pepper

- In a heavy-bottomed casserole, place the peeled and chopped turnips, cut about 1-inch square. Season with salt and pepper ; add the potatoes, also peeled and chopped about the same size as the turnips, season.

- Add the chopped shallots, the bay leaf and thyme, and on top of this add the pricked sausages.

- Sprinkle with the wine or cider, dot with butter, and cover the casserole. Hermetically seal with a paste made from flour and water, brushing this over the joint between the lid and the casserole.

- Cook in a medium hot oven for 2 1/2 to 3 hours. Serve with a purée of apples.

Bar-keeper at Liège

PETIT SALÉ AUX LENTILLES

Pork with lentils, from Flanders

800 g. salt pork
400 g. green lentils
2 l. water
3 carrots
2 onions

2 dl. cream
1 clove
6 peppercorns
bouquet garni*
1 tbsp. strong mustard
salt, pepper

- Soak the salt pork for 24 hours, changing the water frequently.
- In a large saucepan place the pork and add the water, bring slowly to the boil. Add one onion, stuck with the clove, the peppercorns (no salt), and simmer for 2 hours.
- While the pork is cooking, wash the lentils. Cover with cold water, add the chopped onion, carrots and bouquet garni, season lightly with salt and pepper and simmer for 1 1/2 hours. Stir in the cream and mustard.
- Serve the pork surrounded by the lentils.

CÔTES DE PORC ERASME

Pork chops in beer with pasta and cheese, from Brussels

4 pork chops	4 dl. beer
250 g. grated cheese	30 g. butter
300 g. pasta (the larger kind)	salt, pepper

- Sauté the pork chops for 7 minutes on either side in 30 g. butter until they are just cooked.
- In boiling salted water cook the pasta — this should take no more than 8 minutes. Drain.
- Over a low heat, melt the cheese in the beer.
- Place the pasta in a buttered ovenproof dish, put the chops on top, pour the melted cheese and beer over the chops, dot with the remaining butter.
- Brown in the oven for about 15-20 minutes.

CÔTES DE PORC REMOUDOU

Pork chops with cheese and Ardennes ham, from Liège

4 pork chops
4 slices Ardennes ham
4 slices Remoudou cheese
    (Gruyère will do but it is
    not quite the same taste)
50 g. butter

4 dl. dry white wine
1 tsp. strong mustard
2 tbsp. chopped parsley
2 tbsp. chopped chives
salt, pepper

(You will need 4 pieces of silver foil to make an envelope around each chop.)

- Season the chops and cook in the butter until they are golden brown on each side and almost cooked.
- On each piece of foil lay half a slice of ham, half a slice of cheese and one chop. Cover with half a slice of cheese, and half a slice of ham.
- Seal each envelope by pinching all the sides together and place in a very hot oven for 15 minutes.
- Deglaze* the pan in which the chops have been cooked by adding the white wine and scraping up all the crunchy bits that have stuck to the bottom and sides. Add the mustard, parsley and chives, check seasoning, and just before serving, stir in a small piece of butter.

Rue Pierreuse at Liège

CÔTES DE PORC À LA FLAMANDE

Pork chops with apples, from Flanders

4 thick pork chops
    (about 2 inches thick)
50 g. butter
4 large tart apples

2 tbsp. lemon juice
2 crushed juniper berries
salt and pepper
30 g. melted butter
rosemary
2 crushed juniper berries
5 sprigs parsley

- Trim excess fat from the chops, season and brown very gently on both sides in 50 g. butter for 10-15 minutes.

- Put the browned, half-cooked chops in a shallow casserole, sprinkle them with the lemon juice, add parsley, juniper berries and rosemary, and season with salt and pepper.

- Arrange the peeled and sliced apples around and over the chops and pour over the melted butter.

- Cover and cook in a medium to hot oven for 30-35 minutes or until chops are cooked.

- Serve directly from the casserole.

POTÉE D'ARDENNE

A heavy but delicious soup-cum-stew of ham and vegetables

1 kg. Ardennes ham in one piece
3 leeks
3 large carrots
small green cabbage
2 sticks celery
3 large turnips

2 large onions
1 kg. potatoes
2 cloves garlic
bouquet garni*
pepper

- Soak the ham for 24 hours, changing the water frequently.
- Place the ham in a large saucepan and cover with 2 litres of water, bring to the boil and remove the scum with a slotted spoon. Simmer for 1 hour.
- Add the peeled and chopped leeks, carrots, celery, turnips, onions and bouquet garni*, and cook for a further 30 minutes. Add the cabbage, after removing any tough outside leaves and the centre stalk, and chopping roughly. Cook for a further 30 minutes.
- Peel and quarter the potatoes, add to the saucepan and cook until the potatoes are done.
- Serve piping hot.

Street in Blankenberg

GIGOT D'AGNEAU AUX MORILLES

A luxurious dish from the Ardennes : leg of lamb with a sauce of morels and cream

FOR 4-6 PEOPLE

1 leg of lamb	3 shallots
110 g. butter	salt, pepper
1 tbsp. French mustard	nutmeg
2 cloves garlic, cut	1 dl. white wine
into slivers	1 tbsp. butter
500 g. morels	1 dl. cream

- With a small sharp knife make little incisions on both sides of the leg of lamb and insert slivers of garlic into these.
- Melt 50 g. butter and mix in a tbsp. of French mustard and, with a pastry-brush, paint the gigot all over with it.
- Roast for 10 minutes on each side in a very hot oven to brown the lamb, then turn the oven down to medium heat and roast in the usual way, 20 minutes per pound of meat.
- Meanwhile prepare the sauce : wash the morels in several waters then drain and pat them dry in a cloth.
- Sauté the shallots in 60 g. butter. When they change colour, throw in the mushrooms, season with salt, pepper and nutmeg. Cover and stew for 10 minutes.
- When the gigot is done, remove it and keep warm prior to carving it.
- Scrape and pour the gigot pan juices into a saucepan, add the white wine and boil rapidly to brown and reduce the gravy.
- Sprinkle the flour on the morels, mix it in well with a wooden spatula without breaking the mushrooms, pour in the meat gravy and bring to the boil. Mix in the cream and serve the sauce separately in a bowl or large sauceboat.

Lacemakers in Bruges

CASSEROLE D'AGNEAU BRUGEOISE

In this lamb dish from Bruges the meat is not sautéed first

1 kg. boned breast of lamb
125 g. bacon thinly sliced
125 g. Flemish ham (or any
    uncooked ham) thinly sliced
3 onions
3 carrots

1 parsley root
1 2-inch piece of lemon peel
1 sprig thyme
1 bay leaf
1 l. beer
1 tbsp. sugar

- Cut the breast of lamb into 2-inch pieces ; chop the onions, cut the carrots and parsley root into thick rounds.
- Line an ovenproof earthenware casserole with alternate slices of bacon and Flemish ham, add the meat and vegetables. Season with salt and pepper and bury the lemon peel, thyme and bayleaf in the pile. Cover with another layer of alternating bacon and ham.
- Bring the beer to the boil in a saucepan, dilute the sugar in it and pour over the meat.
- Cover the casserole and seal it hermetically with a paste made of flour and water. Cook in a medium oven for 2 hours.

game

CAILLES AUX RAISINS

A delicate, classic way to cook quail

8 quails
30 g. butter
1 tbsp. oil
1 small glass brandy
3 dl. dry white wine

2 tbsp. flour
100 g. seedless white grapes
salt and pepper
juice of 1 lemon

- Clean the quails. Season with salt and pepper. Melt the butter and oil in a heavy-bottomed casserole and sauté the birds until they are golden on all sides. Sprinkle with flour and continue to cook until flour is brown. Add brandy and flambé ; as the flames die down, add wine and lemon juice ; cover and cook over a low heat for 15 to 20 minutes.

- Add the seedless grapes and continue to cook for 5 to 10 minutes more ; check the seasoning.

- Serve on slices of fried bread.

FAISAN À LA BRUXELLOISE

Pheasant with chicory flavoured with juniper berries

1 plump pheasant
2 vine leaves
3 strips fat bacon
small cream cheese (petit suisse)
1 shallot
60 g. butter
1 kg. small chicons (chicory)

1 glass white wine
1 large onion
2 cloves garlic
6 juniper berries
sprig of thyme
1 bay leaf
salt, pepper

(Most shops in Belgium, whether your local poultry shop or supermarket, automatically provide the vine leaves when you buy a pheasant.)

- Clean and dry the pheasant, reserving the liver.
- Chop the shallot, and the liver from the pheasant, and mix with the cream cheese, season with salt and pepper, and stuff the pheasant with this mixture.
- Wrap the vine leaves and the strips of bacon around the pheasant and secure with kitchen string.
- In a heavy-bottomed casserole brown the pheasant on all sides in the butter, remove, and in its place sauté the chopped onion and garlic for 4 minutes without browning.
- Wipe the chicons clean and remove any brown leaves. Add the chicons to the onions and garlic, with the crushed juniper berries, thyme, bay leaf and wine ; season with salt and pepper. Place the pheasant in the middle of the casserole and bring to the boil.
- Cover and cook in a medium to hot oven for 1 hour.
- Serve with mashed potatoes.

Harvest in the region of Gembloux ;
photograph by Maisson, 1884

FAISAN AUX MARRONS

A delicious dish of pheasant and chestnuts, from the Ardennes

1 plump pheasant
3 slices of fat bacon
100 g. butter

500 g. chestnuts
1 glass white wine
salt, pepper

- Clean and dry the pheasant. Wrap in fat bacon and secure with kitchen string. Season. Melt the butter in a casserole and brown the bird on all sides. Cover and continue cooking the pheasant over a very low heat.

- With a knife, make a small incision in all the chestnuts. Place them in a saucepan, cover with cold water, bring to the boil and simmer for 10 minutes. Drain and, when cool enough to handle, remove the shells and brown skin.

- After the pheasant has been slowly cooking for about 50 minutes add the shelled chestnuts, making sure that they get coated with the fat in the casserole, and continue to cook for a further 10 to 15 minutes, or until the bird is cooked.

- Remove the pheasant and chestnuts to a warmed serving dish. Add the white wine to the cooking juices in the casserole, stirring constantly ; add a walnut-sized piece of butter and pour over the pheasant.

GRIVES À LA LIÉGEOISE

Thrushes with juniper berries

(Thrushes are available in Belgian shops, especially poultry shops in the Ardennes ; for some Belgian gourmets they are the most sought-after of all birds, and some even go as far as keeping a special heavy-bottomed casserole just for them, which is never washed but wiped clean after each use.)

4 thrushes
100 g. lean smoked ham, diced
2 tbsp. crushed juniper berries

60 g. butter
2 tbsp. dry white wine
salt, pepper

- Clean the thrushes. Season with salt and pepper.
- In a heavy-bottomed casserole, brown the birds on all sides. Cover and cook over a very low heat for 15 minutes.
- Add the crushed juniper berries, diced ham and white wine, and continue to cook, covered, for a further 10 to 15 minutes, or until done.
- Serve on slices of bread fried in butter until golden.

Hunting at Spa

PIGEONNEAUX AUX LÉGUMES PRIMEURS

Braised pigeons with spring vegetables

4 pigeons
100 g. butter
bunch of young carrots,
   washed and scraped
400 g. shelled fresh peas
400 g. young green beans,
   topped and tailed
12 small onions

12 small new potatoes,
   washed and scraped
1 bay leaf
sprig of thyme
salt, pepper
1 tsp. sugar
1 tbsp. water

- After making sure that the pigeons are clean inside and out, and that you have dried them thoroughly, season the inside of each bird with salt and pepper.

- In a casserole that will hold the birds comfortably melt 100 g. of butter and brown the birds all over.

- Add all the young vegetables, salt and pepper, a teaspoon of sugar and a tablespoon of warm water. Cover with lid and hermetically seal by making a paste of flour and water and brushing this over the joint between the lid and casserole.

- Place in a medium to hot oven for 1 1/4 hours.

- For serving, unless you find the sight of the sealed casserole unappetising, remove the lid at the table with your dinner guests in attendance. The aroma when the lid is first raised is almost as good as the taste of the birds and vegetables themselves.

PERDRIX AU CHOU BLANC

A pot roast of partridges on a bed of white cabbage, from the Ardennes

2 fat partridges
2 vine leaves
4 thin strips of fat bacon
1 white cabbage
200 g. of lean salt bacon in one piece
100 g. melted butter

1 large onion
30 g. dripping or lard
salt, pepper and nutmeg
bouquet garni (2 bay leaves,
sprig of thyme)

(Most shops in Belgium, whether your local poultry shop or supermarket, automatically provide the vine leaves when you buy partridges.)

- Clean and thoroughly dry the birds ; season the insides with salt and pepper. Wrap a vine leaf and two strips of fat bacon around each bird and secure with kitchen string.
- In the melted butter, brown the partridges for 1/2 hour in a medium hot oven.
- While the partridges are cooking, remove the centre stalk from the cabbage and any tough outside leaves, and finely chop.
- In a casserole big enough to take the cabbage and the birds, melt the dripping or lard and gently cook the chopped onion.
- Add the cabbage to the onion and season with salt, pepper and nutmeg. Cover the casserole and, over a very low heat, gently cook the cabbage and onions for 1/2 hour.
- Remove the partridges from the oven after 1/2 hour and place in the centre of the cabbage with the piece of lean bacon, a bouquet garni and a cup of hot water.
- Cover and cook for 1 1/2 hours, either on the top of the stove very gently, or in the oven on a low to medium heat.
- Remove the bouquet garni* and serve with mashed potatoes.

SALMIS DE BÉCASSE

Roast woodcock in a mustard and mushroom sauce, from the Meuse region

4 woodcock
4 tbsp. dry white wine
4 tbsp. rich beef stock*
juice of 2 lemons
1 1/2 tbsp. French mustard

100 g. sliced mushrooms
3 tbsp. butter
1 tbsp. flour
2 tbsp. finely chopped parsley
salt, pepper, nutmeg
beurre manie*

- Clean the woodcock by wiping with a cloth. Roast for 15 minutes in 2 tbsp. butter. The birds will be half cooked.
- Carve, but be sure to do this on a serving dish to catch any blood and juices. Place the carved birds in a large heavy-bottomed frying-pan.
- Crush the livers and giblets into the serving dish with juices ; add dry white wine, beef stock, juice of 2 lemons, mustard, and season to taste with salt, pepper and nutmeg.
- Add the sliced mushrooms and pour this mixture over the woodcock in the frying-pan ; place over a very low heat and cook, stirring so that the pieces do not stick to the pan, and each piece is thoroughly moist.
- Do not let the salmis come to the boil. Just before serving, stir in a beurre manié* made with 1 tbsp. of butter and 1 tbsp. flour.
- Sprinkle with finely chopped parsley and serve.

Above : Hay gatherers ; photograph by Sermois, 1904
Below : Morning chat in Ardennes ; photograph by Herman, 1910

CIVET DE LIÈVRE AUX RAISINS SECS

A rich stew of hare with wine and raisins, from the Ardennes

1 hare (about 2 kg.)	MARINADE
200 g. diced lean bacon	1 1/2 l. red wine
200 g. mushrooms	1 carrot
2 tbsp. oil	1 onion } chopped
small glass of brandy	1 stick celery
30 g. flour	4 cloves garlic, crushed
2 dl. blood	3 bay leaves, 1 sprig thyme
200 g. raisins	salt, peppercorns, cloves

(The blood is essential in this dish ; it is what gives it its strong colour and flavour. Ask your local butcher for the blood ; if he doesn't have the blood from the hare, pig's blood is a very good substitute.)

- Cut the hare into pieces, about 8 in all.

- Put them in an earthenware dish with all the ingredients for the marinade and leave to marinate for 24 hours.

- The next day remove the hare, vegetables and herbs from the marinade, drain and pat dry in a tea-towel.

- In a large casserole sauté the pieces of hare, vegetables, and herbs in the oil, cook until all the pieces are golden brown. Flambé with the brandy, add the flour and continue cooking for a further 3 minutes, or until the flour is soaked up by the oil.

- Add the liquid from the marinade, which you have reduced by a third, by boiling uncovered over a high heat. Place the casserole in a hot oven and cook for 1 1/4 hours.

- Add the raisins and continue to cook for 15 minutes.

- While the hare is cooking, sauté the diced bacon until the fat begins to run, add the sliced mushrooms and cook gently for a further 5 minutes.

- After 1 1/2 hours of cooking, remove casserole from the oven. Extract bay leaves and sprig of thyme.

- Add the bacon, mushrooms and blood and continue to cook on the top of the stove simmering gently for 5 minutes.

Serve either with steamed potatoes or slices of French bread.

SANGLIER SAUCE POIVRADE

Wild boar in a pepper sauce, from Philippeville

1 1/2 kg. wild boar
1 bt. red wine
2 dl. wine winegar
3 slices fat bacon
2 carrots
3 onions
salt

1 stick celery
12 juniper berries
2 cloves
1 tbsp. brown sugar
2 tbsp. flour
16 crushed peppercorns

The boar should be marinated for at least 2 days, but it will be more tender for 4 days marination.

- Chop the celery, carrots, onions and bacon, add the wine, crushed juniper berries, cloves, peppercorns and salt to taste. Marinate the wild boar for 4 days turning frequently.

- Remove the meat and pat dry. Place the vegetables and spices from the marinade in the bottom of a roasting tin and just cover with the marinade sauce. Place the wild board on this bed and pot roast for 2 1/2-3 hours, basting every 15 minutes. Add extra marinade if necessary — the vegetables should be 2/3 covered all the time.

- When the meat is cooked, remove to warmed serving dish and strain the sauce into a medium-sized saucepan.

- Reduce the sauce by a third add the brown sugar and the flour mixed with the cold water ; continue to cook for 5-10 minutes, check seasoning, adding more pepper if desired.

- Pour a small quantity of sauce over the meat and serve the rest separately in a sauceboat.

CHEVREUIL EN CASSEROLE

A rich venison stew, from the Gaume region

1 kg. venison, preferably from the leg
150 g. diced bacon
2 tbsp. flour
1 bt. red wine
1 large onion, chopped
2 tbsp. redcurrant jelly

bouquet garni* (parsley, thyme,
    bay leaf)
salt, freshly ground black
    pepper
juice of 1 lemon

- Wipe and carefully trim the venison, cut into 1-inch squares.
- Sauté the diced bacon until the fat is running. Transfer bacon to a casserole. Add venison to fat in pan and sauté until brown, adding a little oil if necessary. Sprinkle with flour and cook for a further few minutes until the flour has been soaked up by the fat. Transfer the venison to the casserole.
- Add the wine to the pan in which the bacon and venison have been browned. Cook over a high heat, stirring all the brown crusty bits from the sides and bottom of the pan into the wine. Strain over the venison.
- Add the chopped onion, redcurrant jelly, bouquet garni, and lemon juice, and season to taste with salt and freshly ground black pepper.
- Cover the casserole and cook in a medium hot oven for 2 1/2-3 hours.

Serve with a dish of glazed baby carrots or steamed potatoes.

Ruins of the old castle, Laroche

vegetables

ROUSTIQUETTES À LA GRAISSE D'OIE

A fricassée of potatoes and Ardennes ham sautéed in goose fat

1 kg. potatoes
4 thick slices Ardennes ham
1 onion

4 tbsp. goose fat
1 tbsp. chopped parsley
salt, pepper

- Peel the potatoes and put them in a pan of boiling salted water. Remove them when they are only three-quarters cooked, drain them and cut them into thick rounds.
- Chop the onion roughly and the Ardennes ham in bite-sized pieces and sauté them in the goose fat until they take on a little colour.
- Add the potatoes and continue to cook over medium heat, stirring carefully so as not to break them, until they are golden all over and stick to the pan. (The slightly burnt bits that stick to the pan give the dish its name and are greatly prized.)
- Season with a little salt and plenty of coarse black pepper, sprinkle with parsley and serve very hot.

This is a wonderfully tasty dish to go with goose or pork, but may also be served as a luncheon or brunch dish with scrambled eggs and sausages.

FRICASSÉE DE LÉGUMES PRINTANIÈRE

A casserole of spring vegetables, from the Brabant

500 g. baby Brussels sprouts
250 g. new carrots
250 g. baby turnips
250 g. small onions
60 g. butter

2 tbsp. peanut oil
1 tbsp. sugar
1 bay leaf
1 sprig thyme
salt, pepper

- First prepare the vegetables : leave the sprouts, baby turnips and onions whole, peel and trim them. Scrape the carrots and cut them into thick rounds.
- Blanch the sprouts, turnips and carrots in a large pan of salted boiling water for 8-10 minutes. Drain them well.
- Sauté the onions in a deep cast-iron casserole in 30 g. butter and a tbsp. oil. When they start to take on colour, dust them with sugar and cook on a brisk flame for a further 2 minutes, then remove them.
- Add the remaining butter and oil to the pan, and sauté the carrots and turnips in it until they take on colour. Remove them and put the sprouts in their place, adding more butter and oil if necessary.
- When the sprouts have browned a little, add the other vegetables, the bayleaf and sprig of thyme, salt and pepper.
- Start cooking the vegetables over medium heat, stirring carefully and shaking the pan so that the bottom layer does not burn, then after 5 minutes lower the heat, cover the pan and cook gently until the carrots are cooked but still firm.

This is delicious with roast veal or duck.

Market day at Liège, overleaf

RATATOUILLE DU CORON

Nothing to do with the classic French ratatouille, this is a robust potato and cabbage dish from Hainaut.

1 small white cabbage
1 kg. new potatoes
1 onion

2 tbsp. lard
1 l. chicken stock

- Chop the onion and sauté it gently in 1 tbsp. lard until it changes colour.
- Chop the cabbage and potatoes and add them to the onion, stirring well so that they are coated with the lard.
- Pour the chicken stock over the vegetables, bring to the boil, cover and simmer over very low heat for 1 hour.
- Drain the vegetables, mash them together with a fork, add another tablespoon of lard and check the seasoning.

A typical provincial dish from Hainaut. Serve it with pork chops or sausages.

PURÉE ALOSTOISE

An onion purée from Aalst, delicious with roast pork, veal or chicken

500 g. large onions
100 g. butter
1 tbsp. flour

2 dl. milk
nutmeg
salt, pepper

- Peel the onions and quarter them, then cook them in boiling salted water for 10 minutes.
- Drain them and stew them in 40 g. butter until they are very soft, then liquidise them or put them through a fine-meshed sieve.
- Make a roux* with 30 g. butter and 1 tbsp. flour and add the milk to make a light béchamel (see p. 184).
- Add the sieved or liquidised onions, season with salt, pepper and a pinch of nutmeg, and beat in the remaining butter.

Coming home from the fields ; photograph by Sermois, 1905

CÉLERI-RAVE ET POIREAUX AU GRATIN

A dish of baked celeriac and leeks which may be served either as a vegetable course or a starter

300 g. celeriac
250 g. leeks (white part only)
2 eggs
80 g. butter
1 tbsp. flour

2.5 dl. milk
1 egg yolk
nutmeg
salt, pepper
1 tbsp. grated Swiss cheese

- Peel the celeriac and cut it into thin strips about 1 1/2 inches long, then parboil these for a couple of minutes. The strips should remain firm and not be mushy. Take them out and drain.

- Hardboil two eggs for 10 minutes then shell them under cold water and slice them.

- Chop the white part of the leeks and cook this in 30 g. butter for 5-8 minutes. Add the shredded celeriac and continue to cook for a few more minutes. Season with salt and plenty of pepper.

- Make a roux* with the remaining butter and the flour, then add the milk to make a smooth, not too thick béchamel (see p. 184). Season with salt, pepper and a pinch of nutmeg. Away from the heat beat in the egg yolk.

- Arrange one layer of mixed leeks and celeriac in a buttered gratin dish, cover with the sliced eggs then add the remaining vegetables. Spoon the sauce over the lot, sprinkle with the grated cheese and bake in a hot oven until gratinéed.

Shepherd and his fold in Laeken park

CHOU ROUGE À L'AIGRE-DOUX

Braised sweet-and-sour red cabbage with apples — a Flemish recipe

1 large red cabbage
4 tbsp. lard or goose fat
2 tbsp. wine vinegar
2 tbsp. sugar
0.5 dl. water

2 cloves
salt, pepper
3 tbsp. redcurrant jelly
2 sour apples

- Shred the cabbage finely, discarding the thick inner stalk and any discoloured outer leaves, then put it in an ovenproof casserole dish.
- In a saucepan put the lard or goose fat, the vinegar, water, sugar, salt, pepper and cloves ; bring to the boil and pour over the cabbage in the casserole.
- Put the casserole in a preheated medium oven for 2 hours, checking every now and then to see whether you need to add a little more water.
- Peel and core the apples and cut them into thick wedges.
- About 20 minutes before the 2 hours are up, add the apples to the casserole, and dilute the redcurrant jelly in the cooking juices.
- Serve the braised red cabbage with roast goose, duck or pork.

Above : Place Royale, Brussels
Below : Le Pavillon de la Laiterie in the Bois de la Cambre, Brussels

CHICONS À LA TERNAT

A vegetable casserole that doubles up as a robust luncheon dish

1 kg. chicons (chicory)
80 g. butter
juice of 1 lemon
2 large onions
2 shallots

200 g. streaky bacon in one piece
500 g. new potatoes, cooked
salt, pepper
nutmeg (optional)
1 tbsp. chopped parsley

- Melt 25 g. of butter in a deep pan, add the chicons (left whole), sprinkle with the lemon juice and a little salt and stew gently until they are cooked but still firm.
- Drain them and pat dry in a cloth, then brown them quickly in another 25 g. of butter.
- Chop the shallots and onions finely and dice the bacon. Sauté all this in 30 g. of butter, add the cooked potatoes and brown the whole mixture.
- Put all the vegetables and bacon in a casserole dish, season with salt, pepper and nutmeg (optional) and sprinkle with parsley.

MOUSSELINE BRABANÇONNE

A purée of Brussels sprouts with cream

1 kg. small young Brussels sprouts
2 shallots
50 g. butter
juice of 1/2 lemon

1 dl. cream
salt, pepper
nutmeg

GARNISH
Croûtons of bread fried in butter and oil

- Cook the sprouts in salted boiling water until tender, then drain, reserving a little of the juice.
- Chop the shallots and melt them in 25 g. butter until transparent.
- Put the sprouts in a liquidiser, add the shallots, lemon juice, salt, pepper, and a pinch of nutmeg, and blend to a thick purée, adding if necessary a spoonful of the vegetable cooking liquid.
- Pour the purée into a bowl, add the remaining butter and the cream, and serve garnished with croûtons fried in a mixture of butter and oil.

FRICASSÉE DE CHAMPIGNONS À L'ARDENNAISE

Possible only during a very short season, this is one of the best ways to cook wild mushrooms.

500 g. mixed wild mushrooms
    (chanterelles, pleurotes, cornes
    d'abondance, mousserons, etc.)
2 slices Ardennes ham
2 shallots
80 g. butter

0.5 dl. fruity but dry white wine
    (such as a Moselle)
1/2 tbsp. each of chopped
    parsley, chives, tarragon
    and chervil
salt, pepper

- Wash the mushrooms several times in vinegared water, drain and dry in a cloth.
- Chop the shallots, shred the ham. Melt 50 g. of butter in a wide saucepan and sauté the shallots in it for 2 minutes, then add the ham and cook together, stirring with a wooden spoon until they take on colour. Add the mushrooms and sauté for a further 2-3 minutes.
- Add the white wine, season with salt and pepper and cook uncovered over medium heat until all the liquid has evaporated.
- Stir in 30 g. butter and the herbs and cook, stirring, over a high flame until the mushrooms have browned.

This is a perfect foil for roast veal or lamb and may also be eaten as a first course.

MORILLES AU POIVRE VERT

One of the most delicious ways of cooking morels, a dish from Namur

500 g. fresh morels
2 shallots
50 g. butter
salt

1 tbsp. soft green peppercorns
juice of 1/2 lemon
1 dl. thick cream

- Wash the morels carefully in vinegared water after trimming the stalks, drain and pat them dry in a cloth.
- Cut the larger ones in two, leave the small ones whole. Chop the shallots finely.
- Melt the butter in a thick-bottomed frying-pan and sauté the shallots in it for 2 minutes. Add the morels and fry them over fairly brisk heat until they begin to give out moisture. Lower the heat, add the salt and peppercorns and stew the mushrooms gently until they are tender and the liquid has evaporated.
  Morels, considered the Queen of mushrooms, are indigestible if not thoroughly cooked, so make sure that they are soft, not springy.
- Sprinkle the lemon juice over the morels, then pour in the thick cream, taking care that it does not curdle.
- Serve very hot, with steak or a roast.

POIRES AU LARD

A delicious country recipe from Limbourg that uses dried pears

500 g. dried pears
125 g. streaky bacon in one piece
1 tbsp. lard
1 large onion

1 bouquet garni*
6 peppercorns
3 cloves
water

- Soak the dried pears in warm water for 30 minutes, then drain them well and pat them dry in a cloth.
- Chop the onion finely ; dice the bacon.
- Sauté the onion and bacon in the lard until they change colour.
- Quarter the pears and add them to the onion and bacon. Cook them gently, stirring for a further two minutes, then pour enough water to cover, add the bouquet garni, peppercorns and cloves, bring to the boil and simmer uncovered until most of the juice has evaporated.

This is good with goose, duck or pork and may also be an unusual accompaniment to game.

Woman selling milk, Liège

stocks and sauces

COURT-BOUILLON

A basic bouillon with multiple uses

1/2 l. water
1/2 l. dry white wine
1 tbsp. white wine vinegar
2 carrots, peeled and sliced
1 leek, trimmed, peeled and sliced
2 shallots, peeled and sliced

12 lightly crushed black peppercorns
2 parsley stalks
1 sprig thyme
2 bay leaves
1/2 tsp. salt

In a large saucepan, place all ingredients and bring to the boil. Simmer for half an hour. The bouillon is now ready for whatever recipe you are following.

CHICKEN STOCK

Worth making and stocking ready for use

2 chicken carcases, including giblets
2 carrots, peeled and sliced
2 onions, peeled and sliced
1 leek, trimmed, washed and sliced

1 bay leaf
sprig thyme
3 parsley stalks
4 black peppercorns
1/2 tsp. salt

- Break the carcases into pieces and place them, with the giblets, in a large saucepan. Cover with cold water and add the remaining ingredients.

- Bring slowly to the boil, skimming off any scum with a slotted spoon. Cover, reduce the heat and simmer for 2 hours, adding more water if level drops below that of the bones. Remove from the heat, strain and allow to cool. Skim off any fat.

Stock freezes well, and there is no comparison between homemade stock and stock cubes. Pour the stock, in usable quantities, into rigid containers. Cover, seal and freeze. Alternatively, the strained stock may be reduced by boiling briskly, cooled and frozen in ice cube trays. When frozen, transfer the cubes to polythene bags, seal and return to freezer.

VEAL STOCK

One of the most useful things to have in the deep-freeze

1 kg. knuckle of veal
2 carrots, peeled and sliced
2 onions, peeled and sliced
1 leek, trimmed, washed and sliced

1 bay leaf
1 sprig of thyme
3 parsley stalks
4 white peppercorns

- Chop the knuckle into pieces and place them in a large saucepan. Cover with water and add the remaining ingredients.
- Bring slowly to the boil, skimming off any scum with a slotted spoon. Cover, reduce the heat and simmer for 2 hours, adding more water if level drops below that of the bones. Remove from heat, strain and allow to cool.

Stock freezes well, and there is no comparison between homemade stock and stock cubes. Pour the stock, in usable quantities, into rigid containers. Cover, seal and freeze.
Alternatively the strained stock may be reduced by boiling briskly, cooled and frozen in ice cube trays.
When frozen transfer the cubes to polythene bags, seal and return to freezer.

BEEF STOCK

The basis of good brown sauces

1 1/2 kg. shin or neck of beef
3 carrots, peeled and sliced
2 onions, peeled and sliced
1 leek, trimmed, washed and sliced
1 celery stalk, washed and sliced
1 bay leaf

1 sprig fresh thyme
2 parsley stalks
1/2 tsp. salt
2 cloves
5 black peppercorns

- Chop the shin or neck into pieces and place them in a large saucepan. Cover with cold water and add the remaining ingredients.
- Bring slowly to the boil, skimming any scum with a slotted spoon. Cover, reduce the heat and simmer gently for at least 3 hours, adding more water if level drops below that of the bones. Remove from heat, strain and allow to cool. Skim off any fat.

See recipe above for freezing the stock.

SAUCE BÉCHAMEL

The basic white sauce of classic cuisine

3 dl. milk
1 small onion, peeled
   and roughly chopped
1 carrot, peeled and sliced
1 small stick of celery,
   washed and sliced

1 bay leaf
3 peppercorns
25 g. butter
25 g. cornflour
salt and freshly ground black
   pepper

- Place the milk, onion, carrot, celery, bay leaf and peppercorns in a saucepan, bring to the boil and remove from heat. Cover the pan and leave to infuse for 20 minutes, then strain.

- Melt the butter in a saucepan and stir in the cornflour. Cook gently for 3 minutes, stirring constantly. Remove from the heat and gradually add the strained milk, stirring briskly until sauce is smooth. Return to the heat, bring to the boil, then reduce heat and simmer for 5 to 10 minutes to ensure that the flour is cooked. Add seasoning to taste.

MAYONNAISE

An important feature of Belgian cooking

3 egg yolks
1/4 l. olive oil
1/2 tsp. salt

wine vinegar,
or the juice of 1/2 lemon

- Whisk the egg yolks thoroughly, add the salt and the olive oil drop by drop. This is very important, and you should make sure that you have whisked in each drop of oil before adding the next. Once the mayonnaise begins to thicken you can add larger drops. When you have incorporated half the oil, add a few drops of wine vinegar or lemon juice. The mayonnaise will be much thinner in consistency now, and you can add the rest of the oil in a steady stream, whisking all the time until all the oil is incorporated. Taste, and if required, add more salt and a drop of vinegar.

Mayonnaise using a liquidiser

3 medium-sized eggs, whites as well
1/2 tsp. salt

1 tsp. lemon juice or wine vinegar
1/4 l. olive oil

- Put the eggs, salt, and 4 tbsp. olive oil into the liquidiser, mix for 4 seconds with the machine running. Add half of the olive oil in a steady flow. The mayonnaise should be very thick now. Add the lemon juice or wine vinegar, mix for 2 seconds.
- Trickle the rest of the oil into the mayonnaise with the machine running.
- Taste, if required add more salt and lemon juice ; mix for a further 2 seconds.

Bathing in the Meuse

desserts

TIMBALE DE POIRES

A hot pear pudding from the Namur region

500 g. pears
200-250 g. thin slices bread
(not too fresh)
125 g. butter, melted

100 g. fine-grained brown
sugar
1 dl. water

- Butter a charlotte mould (a plain deep round mould with sloping sides).
- Remove the crusts from the bread and line the mould with them. Spoon a little melted butter over.
- Peel, core and slice the pears thinly and spread a layer of pears over the bread. Dust with sugar and brush with a little melted butter.
- Cover with another layer of bread and repeat until you have filled the mould.
- Finally, pour the dl. of water over the lot, and bake in a medium oven for 1 hour.
- Unmould and serve hot with thin fresh cream.

RIJSTPAP

A saffron-flavoured Flemish rice-pudding

300 g. rice
2 l. milk
100 g. brown sugar (or more)

1 stick cinnamon
saffron

- Put the rice in the milk with the brown sugar and cinnamon. Bring to the boil, then turn the heat down and simmer very gently with the lid on until the rice is very soft.
- Add a strong pinch of saffron and more sugar to taste, stir well and turn out onto flat plates, spreading it out well.
- Allow to cool and sprinkle with brown sugar before serving.

Flemish milkmaid

PAIN PERDU AU CRAMIQUE

A nursery and supper favourite that uses leftover raisin bread

leftover cramique cut in
    slices (see p. 203)
1/2 l. milk
100 g. sugar
1/2 tsp. powdered cinnamon

redcurrant jam or jelly
2 eggs, lightly beaten
sugar
butter

- Cut medium-thick slices of slightly dry cramique.

- Heat the milk with the sugar and cinnamon.

- Dip each slice in the milk then spread it with redcurrant jam or jelly and cover it with another slice similarly treated.

- Dip the sandwich in the beaten eggs, sprinkle with sugar and fry lightly in foaming butter until it is golden all over.

PRUNEAUX À LA GUEUZE

Prunes stewed in beer, a Brussels dessert

500 g. prunes, soaked in
    water for 2 hours
0.5 l. Gueuze (or similar beer)

1 stick cinnamon
100-125 g. sugar,
    according to taste

- Drain the prunes and put them in a saucepan with the beer, cinnamon and sugar.

- Cook until the prunes are soft.

- Remove the cinnamon stick, drain the prunes and put them in a bowl.

- Boil the syrup until thick and pour over the prunes.

- Chill for at least 8 hours and serve as a compote by itself or with a cinnamon-flavoured rice pudding.

Family group

TARTE À LA RHUBARBE

A Flemish rhubarb pie

FOR THE FILLING
500 g. rhubarb
200 g. sugar
0.5 dl. water

FOR THE PASTRY
500 g. flour
125 g. butter
2 eggs
1 dl. milk
10 g. yeast

- Peel and cut the rhubarb into 2-inch pieces and blanch these in boiling water for 2 minutes, then drain.
- Make a syrup with 200 g. sugar and 0.5 dl. water. When the syrup starts to change colour, throw in the rhubarb and cook it for a few minutes, stirring constantly so that it does not stick. Allow to cool.
- Now make the pastry: mix together the flour and the eggs, work in the butter, milk and yeast. Knead until the dough is smooth and resilient. Cover with a cloth and leave in a cool place for 1 hour.
- Roll out the dough, line a pie-dish with it, add the filling and bake in a moderate oven for 30 minutes.

Flemish milkmaid

OMELETTE AUX POMMES

A delicious sweet omelette, from the Ardennes

6 eggs
0.5 dl. milk
2 apples

100 g. sugar
60 g. butter
2 tbsp. brandy

- Beat the eggs lightly, with a fork, with the milk and 75 g. sugar.
- Peel and core the apples and cut them into thin wedges.
- Sauté the apples in the butter until they are golden, then add the egg mixture to the fryingpan and cook in the usual way.
- When the omelette is done, fold it, pour the warmed brandy over it and flambé.
- Sprinkle with a little more sugar and serve very hot.

MOUSSE AUX NOIX

A walnut mousse, from Bastogne

250 g. shelled dried walnuts
1 dl. mandarin liqueur
    (if unavailable, substitute
    an orange-flavoured liqueur
    such as curaçao)
30 g. butter
30 g. flour

1/2 l. milk
100 g. sugar
4 eggs
0.5 dl. cream
a few chopped walnuts
    for decoration

- Soak the walnuts in mandarin (or orange-flavoured) liqueur for 1 hour, then put them in the liquidiser and blend at high speed to obtain a smooth paste.
- Make a roux* with the butter and flour and whisk in the milk gradually as for a béchamel (see p. 184). When the sauce is thick and smooth, beat in 100 g. sugar.
- Separate the egg yolks from the whites.
- Beat in the egg yolks one by one into the sweet béchamel and mix in the walnut purée and cream. Adjust the sugar content if necessary.
- Beat the egg whites till stiff and fold them delicately into the walnut mixture.
- Turn the mousse into long glasses or individual ramekins and chill for at least 6 hours.
- Decorate the top with a few chopped nuts just before serving.

Above : Ploughing the fields ; photograph by Herman, 1912
Below : Washerwomen by the Semois at Bouillon, 1913

COMPOTE DE FRUITS ROUGES LIMBOURGEOISE

Cherries, strawberries and raspberries in red wine, a refreshing summer dessert

FOR 4-6 PEOPLE

500 g. cherries
500 g. strawberries
250 g. raspberries
1 l. red wine

250 g. sugar
zest of 1/4 lemon
2 cloves
nutmeg

- Remove the stalks from the cherries and put them in a very deep saucepan with the wine, sugar, lemon and spices.
- Bring to the boil and simmer for 2 minutes then turn the heat off and allow the cherries to cool in the liquid (this will ensure that they continue to cook a little).
- While the liquid is still warm, add the strawberries and raspberries and let them macerate in the spiced wine until it has cooled down completely.
- Remove the lemon peel and cloves and chill for at least 6 hours before serving with a jug of cream.

BOULES AUX MARRONS

Sweet chestnut croquettes, from Belgian Luxembourg

500 g. sweet chestnut purée
60 g. butter
3 eggs

60 g. sugar
100 g. breadcrumbs
oil for frying

- Separate the egg whites from the yolks.
- Cream the butter, egg yolks and sugar together and work this mixture into the chestnut purée, then chill it for 2 hours.
- Beat the egg whites till stiff.
- Shape the chestnut mixture into small bands, dip each ball into the egg whites, roll in breadcrumbs and deepfry in oil.

You can serve these chestnut croquettes as they are or, if you have a very sweet tooth, you may serve them with a syrup made of honey and water.

FRAISES AU FROMAGE ROSE

A dessert of cream cheese and strawberries, from Namur

1 kg. strawberries
sugar to taste
2 oranges
300 g. cream cheese

1 dl. orange liqueur
   (such as curaçao)
2 egg yolks

- Remove the strawberry stalks and put half the fruit in a bowl. Dust with sugar and press the juice of 2 oranges over them and half the orange liqueur.
- Put the remaining strawberries in a liquidiser with sugar to taste and blend into a purée.
- Beat the cream cheese so that it softens, fold in the strawberry purée and more sugar to taste, beat in two egg yolks and, finally, the rest of the orange liqueur.
- Arrange the cream cheese in the centre of a deep bowl and pile up the marinated strawberries all around it. Chill for 6-8 hours.
- Serve with dry dessert biscuits.

Cheese-seller at Liège

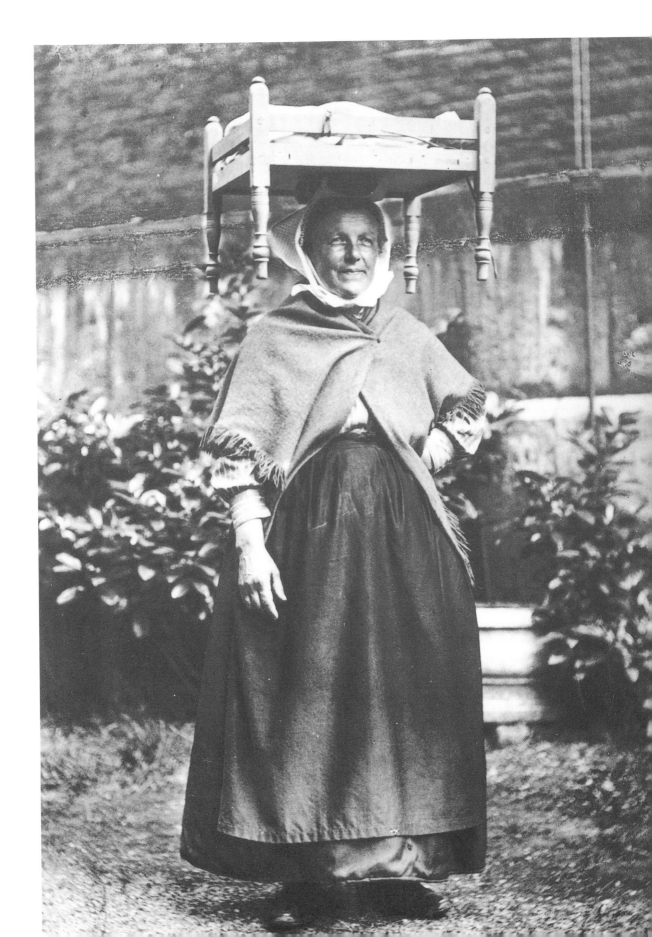

breads and biscuits

PAIN D'ÉPICES

A tea-time favourite all over Belgian : sweet spiced bread

250 g. plain flour
200 g. liquid honey
50 g. brown sugar
2 tbsp. beer

1 tsp. brown sugar
pinch of cinnamon
pinch of ground cloves
1 tsp. bicarbonate of soda

- In a saucepan, melt the honey and sugar together.

- In a large bowl, sieve together the flour, the bicarbonate of soda, cinnamon and ground cloves. Make a well in the centre of the flour, pour the honey and sugar mixture in, and work together until you have a fairly wet dough ; add a drop of water, if necessary.

- Now the work begins : knead and pull and push for at least 10 minutes (we were told until your arms get tired, but we both started to flag after 3 minutes and this just isn't long enough).

- Let the dough rest in a cool place for 2 days, then hold another session of kneading and pulling for 10 minutes.

- Half fill a small buttered bread tin, brush with a mixture of beer and sugar and bake in a hot oven for 45 to 60 minutes.

If you have a food processor this can all be done by machine.

CRAMIQUE

Raisin bread

500 g. plain flour	1 dl. warm milk
200 g. butter	25 g. yeast
150 g. brown sugar	pinch cinnamon
250 g. currants	salt
3 eggs	

- Sieve the flour, pinch of cinnamon and pinch of salt into a large mixing bowl.

- Blend the yeast and warm milk together. Mix flour and milk mixture together, cover and leave to rise in a warm place for 1 hour.

- Add the melted butter, eggs, sugar, and raisins and work together kneading and pulling for at least 10 to 15 minutes, or until the dough is smooth and elastic and leaves the bowl clean.

- Place in a buttered bread tin, pressing down slightly so that the dough touches the sides ; the dough should half fill the tin. Leave to rise for 2 hours, or until the dough reaches the top of the tin.

- Bake in a hot oven for 1 hour.

SPECULOOS

A delicious light biscuit to be found all over Belgium

500 g. self-raising flour
200 g. butter
2 eggs

375 g. brown sugar
1 tsp. bicarbonate of soda

- In a large mixing bowl, cream the butter and sugar together until pale and fluffy. Add the eggs and mix well. Next, sieve the flour and bicarbonate of soda into the bowl and work all the ingredients together.
- The dough should come away from the bowl cleanly and not stick to your fingers ; add a little water or flour if it is too dry or too sticky.
- This biscuit mixture is best if left covered in the refrigerator overnight, but if this is not convenient, chill in the refrigerator for at least 1/2 hour.
- Roll out the pastry and shape your biscuits, using a speculoos mould (a small glass will do just as well).
- Bake on a well-greased baking tray in a low to medium hot oven for 20 to 25 minutes, or until your biscuits are cooked.

This is one of the basic recipes, but you will find that each region has its own, adding either cinnamon, ground ginger or ground cloves — experiment and see which you prefer, adding all three if you like.

GAUFRES DE BRUXELLES

Waffles

100 g. self-raising flour
100 g. melted butter
4 egg yolks
1/4 l. milk

pinch of salt
1/2 sachet vanilla sugar
8 egg whites

- Sieve the flour into a large mixing bowl.
- Mix together the flour, melted butter, milk, egg yolks, salt and vanilla sugar.
- When these are well mixed, add the lightly beaten egg whites and leave for 1 hour.
- Cook in a waffle iron. Serve with a sprinkling of sugar and fresh whipped cream.

PALETS BRUGEOIS

A light melt-in-the-mouth biscuit

125 g. brown sugar
125 g. softened butter
3 eggs

125 g. self-raising flour
100 g. sultanas
2 tbsp. rum

- Soak the sultanas in the rum for half an hour before starting your biscuits.
- In a large bowl beat together the eggs, softened butter and brown sugar until smooth.
- Add the sifted flour and sultanas and work the mixture thoroughly, using a wooden spoon, until smooth.
- Place the mixture in a piping-bag, and using a large rose nozzle, pipe small stars onto a greased baking tray, making sure that you leave enough room between them so that they can rise and spread.
- Cook in a medium-hot oven for 15-20 minutes, or until cooked.

drinks and preserves

BIÈRE DE MÉNAGE

Home-made beer

50 g. hopshoots
250 g. pearl barley
2 tsp. chicory grains

10 g. yeast
12 l. water
175 g. sugar

- Bring to the boil the 12 l. of water and add the barley, chicory and hops, which you have placed in a small muslin bag. Boil for 1 1/2 hours. Remove the muslin bag, add the sugar and continue to boil for 1/2 hour.
- Let your beer cool and when it is lukewarm add the yeast, which should also be in a muslin bag as this makes it easier to remove. Leave the beer in a warm room for 24 hours.
- Remove the yeast, skim the froth from the top of the beer. Place in bottles and keep in a cool place.
  Wait three days before drinking. But don't keep for too long or the bottles might explode, as the fermentation continues even after the removal of the yeast.

HOT CHOCOLATE

A basic recipe for a nursery favourite

200 g. chocolate
1 l. milk

1 sachet vanilla sugar
6 tbsp. thick cream

- Break the chocolate into small pieces and melt in 6 tbsp. milk, add the rest of the milk and vanilla sugar, bring to the boil twice.
- Pour into 4 cups and top with thick cream, which you have beaten so that it stands on its own.

You can add grated chocolate to decorate if you like.

CAFÉ LIÉGEOIS

Cold coffee and cream

FOR 4 CUPS
2 cups strong cold black coffee
2 cups fresh cream

50 g. whipped cream
grated chocolate to decorate

- Mix the coffee and fresh cream together, pour into cups or glasses, spoon whipped cream on top and sprinkle with grated chocolate.

MAITRANK

A beautifully light mixture of champagne and white wine flavoured with sweet woodruff

FOR 15 PEOPLE
(the day before)

5 litres wine (Moselle)
1 bottle Champagne
1 glass brandy
small handful of sweet woodruff
without their roots

2 oranges, sliced
sugar if liked

- Mix all the ingredients together and leave for 24 hours in a cool place. It's even better if left for 3 or 4 days.
- Serve very cold.

*Coal-carrier,
Liège*

RAISINS À L'EAU DE VIE

Grapes preserved in alcohol

1 1/2 kg. muscat grapes	**300 g. sugar**
1 l. eau de vie or brandy	

- The grapes must be as near perfect as possible. Remove the stalks, wash in cold water and gently dry in a tea towel.
- Using only grapes with undamaged skins, place in one-litre preserving jar. Keep at least 400 g. to one side (these grapes do not have to be in such good condition).
- Press the 400 g. of grapes through a fine sieve to get at least 2 dl. grape juice. Put the juice in an enamel pan with the sugar and cook until you have a thick syrup. Allow to cool completely, then add the eau de vie or brandy and pour over the grapes.
- Seal the jar well and keep in a cool place ; don't disturb for at least 4 weeks.

PRUNES À L'AIGRE-DOUX

Damsons in vinegar, from the Ardennes

1 kg. damsons	**3 cloves**
1 l. wine vinegar	**5 peppercorns**
500 g. sugar	**stick cinnamon**
	salt

- Wash and dry the damsons and remove the stalks. Using a sewing needle carefully prick the skins, to prevent them from bursting when they are boiled.
- In an enamel saucepan, place the vinegar, sugar, cloves, cinnamon and peppercorns. Bring the vinegar to the boil and add the damsons. Boil for 5 minutes and remove the damsons with a slotted spoon.
- Add a pinch of salt and boil the liquid for a further 10 minutes. Remove the spices, pour the vinegar over the plums and leave covered in a cool place for 24-48 hours.
- Drain the damsons, bring the liquid to the boil once more, arrange the fruit in a preserving jar, cover with the vinegar and seal.

Wait at least four weeks before using.

glossary

al dente	To cook vegetables or pasta until just cooked (they should retain a bite in them).
au naturel	Food preserved in its own juices without the addition of artificial colouring or acids.
bard	To cover meat, poultry, game and sometimes fish with thin strips of pork fat or unsmoked bacon before roasting or braising.
baste	To pour or spoon liquid over food as it cooks in order to moisten and flavour it.
batter	Something that is beaten. Usually means the mixture from which pancakes, puddings and cakes are made. The batter used for pancakes and for coating purposes is made of eggs, flour and milk (sometimes water or beer) and is fairly liquid in consistency.
beat	To mix with a spoon, spatula, whisk, rotary beater or electric blender ; to make a mixture smooth and light by enclosing air.
beurre manié	Equal quantities of butter and flour kneaded together and added bit by bit to a stew, casserole or sauce to thicken it.
bind	To thicken soups or sauces with eggs, cream, etc.
blanch	To preheat in boiling water or steam. This can be done for different reasons : to loosen outer skins of fruits, nuts and vegetables ; to whiten veal, chicken or sweetbreads ; to remove excess salt or bitter flavour from bacon, ham, sprouts, turnips, endive, etc. ; to prepare fruits and vegetables for freezing or preserving.
blend	To mix two or more ingredients thoroughly.
boil	To cook in any liquid — usually water, wine or stock, or a combination of the three — brought to boiling point and kept there.
bone	To remove the bones from fish, poultry or game.
boudin	Blood sausage.
bouquet garni	Bunch of herbs, used to flavour stews, casseroles and sauces. Usually consisting of parsley, thyme, garlic and bay leaves, tied together with kitchen string.
chop	To cut into very small pieces with a sharp knife or a chopper.
cream	To work one or more foods with a heavy spoon or a firm spatula until the mixture is soft and creamy.
croûte	A pastry case for beef, lamb, ham or pâté.
croûton	Bread trimmed of crusts and cut into shapes sautéed in oil or butter, sometimes rubbed with garlic.
deglaze	To detach the juices and all the particles which have adhered to the bottom and sides of a saucepan in which food was cooked. This is done by adding wine, stock, water or cream.
gratin	To cook « au gratin » is to brown food in the oven — usually covered in a sauce and dotted with breadcrumbs, cheese and butter — until a crisp, golden coating forms.

haricots princesse	Very small thin green beans.
grill	To cook by direct heat such as an open fire, charcoal, gas or electricity.
julienne	Cut into fine strips the length of a matchstick.
knead	To work dough with hands until it is of the desired elasticity or consistency.
lard	To lard, process by which small strips of pork fat or unsmoked bacon are threaded through meat, poultry or game to add moisture and flavour.
liaison	To thicken a sauce, gravy or stew : either by adding flour, cornflour, arrowroot, rice flour or a beurre manié (flour and butter) ; or by stirring in egg yolk or double cream. For some dishes blood is used.
marinade	A highly flavoured liquid — usually red or white wine or olive oil, or a combination of the two — seasoned with carrots, onion, bay leaf, herbs and spices. The purpose of a marinade is to flavour the food and soften the fibres of tougher foods.
marinate	To let food stand or steep in a marinade. See above.
mince	To reduce to very small particles with a mincer, chopper or knife.
parboil	To precook, or boil until partially cooked.
poach	To cook gently in simmering (not boiling) liquid.
quenelle	The finely pounded flesh of fish, shellfish, veal, poultry, game liver, mixed with egg whites and cream, and pounded to a velvety smooth paste. These feather-light dumplings are then poached in a light stock or salted water.
reduce	To cook a sauce over a high heat, uncovered, until it is reduced by evaporation to the desired consistency. This culinary process improves both flavour and appearance.
roast	To cook meat by direct heat on a spit or in the oven.
roux	The gentle amalgamation of butter and flour over a low heat ; capable of absorbing at least six times its own weight when cooked.
salmis	To cook jointed poultry or game in a rich wine sauce after it has been roasted until almost ready.
sauté	To fry lightly in a small amount of hot butter or oil, shaking the pan or turning food frequently during cooking.
sear	To brown and seal the surface of meat quickly over high heat. This prevents juices from escaping.
simmer	To cook in liquid just below boiling point, with small bubbles rising gently to the surface.
steam	To cook food in vapour over boiling water.
wild mushrooms	chanterelles, pleurotes, cornes d'abondance, mousserons and all wild mushrooms with their own distinctive flavour.
zest	The finely grated rind of lemon and orange.

measurements - oven temperatures

Metric		British		American
30 g.	=	1 oz.	=	2 tbsp
120 g.	=	4 oz.	=	1/2 cup
240 g.	=	8 oz.	=	1 cup
480 g.	=	16 oz.	=	2 cups

NB. — 1 oz is nearer 28 grams but to make conversion easier we have rounded it up to 30 grams.

Metric		British		American
1 dl.	=	1/5 pt.	=	1/2 cup
3 dl.	=	1/2 pt.	=	1 1/4 cups
6 dl.	=	1 pt.	=	2 1/2 cups

NB. — 1000 ml. = 100 cl. = 10 dl. = 1 litre.

Fahrenheit	Gas Mark	Centigrade	Heat of Oven
225° F	1/4	110° C	very cool
250° F	1/2	130° C	very cool
275° F	1	140° C	cool
300° F	2	150° C	cool
325° F	3	170° C	warm
350° F	4	180° C	warm
375° F	5	190° C	fairly hot
400° F	6	200° C	fairly hot
425° F	7	220° C	hot
450° F	8	230° C	very hot
475° F	9	240° C	very hot

comparative meatcuts

beef

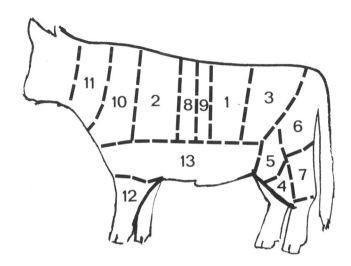

1. sirloin	filet pur	filetstuk
2. forerib	entrecôte	tussenrib
3. rump	petite tête	kleinhoofd
4. top rump	aiguilette	naaldje
5. topside	tranche grasse	dikke bil
6. silverside	filet d'anvers	filet d'anvers
7. silverside	tache noire	zwarte plek
8. back rib	faux filet	valse filet
9. back rib	petit nerf	zenuwstuk
10. blade and chuck	pointe d'épaule	pelure
11. neck	collier	nek
12. shin	gite à la noix	kookvlees
13. brisket and flank	poitrine	kookvlees

1. Sirloin is the cut from which the famous T-bone steaks come. The meat is tender and lean ; more often than not, it is cut into steaks.

2. Forerib is the cut from which the classic roast rib of beef comes. By leaving the meat on the bone, you retain all te flavour and juices. You can buy rib-steaks, which are excellent grilled.

3. Rump, usually cut into steaks for frying or grilling, also makes an excellent joint for roasting.

4. Top rump, rolled and tied, should be slow-roasted or braised. It is sometimes cut into steaks for braising.

5. Topside, lean and fine-grained, may be slow-roasted or braised.

6. and 7. Silverside has a very good flavour and may be slow roasted, poached or braised. Also a very good joint for salting.

8. and 9. Backrib, another good cut for slow-roasting. Boned, rolled and tied, the joint may also be pot-roasted or braised.

10. Chuck and blade, fairly lean cuts that need moist, slow cooking, are ideal for stews and casseroles.

11. Neck and clod are usually prepared by the butcher for mince.

12. Meat from the shin is interlarded with gelatinous tissues which melt down during cooking to give rich juices, making this cut ideal for long, slow, moist cooking such as a daube.

13. Brisket and flank are the classic cuts for salting, but either salted or fresh they are at their best poached. They are long, flat pieces of meat, interspersed with fat which helps give them their good flavour.

veal

1. leg	cuisse de veau	kalfsbil
2. loin and rump	carré or selle	koteletten
3. shoulder	épaule	schouder
4. best end of neck	basses côtes	lage ribben
5. breast and flank	poitrine and tendron	ragout
6. knuckle and shin	jarret	knukle
7. neck	collier	kalfsnek

1. The leg is divided into joints for roasting or braising ; the lower part of the leg (the flank) also provides small but very tender escalopes.

2. The loin is very tender and lean, and the chops can be grilled, roasted or fried. When boned and rolled it makes a first class joint for roasting. The rump is a prime cut that may be roasted, grilled or fried ; it is usually sliced into thick medallions.

3. Veal shoulder has its enthusiasts, like shoulder of lamb. The meat is sweet and tender, but there is more muscle and fat on it than on the leg. Most butchers will bone and roll this joint for you, ready for roasting or braising.

4. Best end of neck. The meat of the central ribs is usually cut into chops for grilling or roasting ; if grilled, the lean meat needs basting.

5. The breast is very bony, muscular and interlarded with fat and membrane. It is mainly used for stews and casseroles, but when boned, rolled and stuffed it makes an unusual joint fort poaching or braising.

6. Knuckle and shin are both sinewy, well-flavoured cuts that need moist cooking. Meat from the shin and the knuckle may be poached or braised. The famous dish « osso buco » is usually taken from the knuckle (the hind leg), which has more meat around the bone than the shin (foreleg), which is usually cut up for stews and casseroles.

7. The neck is usually prepared by the butcher, either for stews and casseroles or for mince.

8. Calf's feet are very rich in gelatin. A split calf's foot will give 1/2 litre of firm jelly when simmered in liquid.

lamb

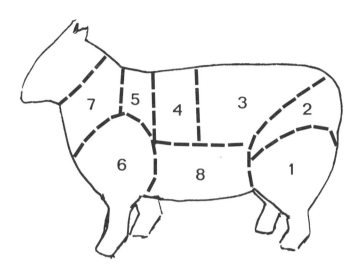

1. leg	gigot	lamsbout
2. filet end of leg	bas de gigot	lamsbout
3. loin or chump chops	côtes au filet	filetkoteletten
4. best-end of neck	côtelettes	koteletten
5. middle neck chops	basses côtes	karbonaden
6. shoulder	épaule	schouder
7. scrag-end of neck	collier	lamsnek
8. breast	ragoût	ragout

1. et 2. The most popular joints for roasting, the leg has a high proportion of lean, tender meat to a very small proportion of bone. The leg is either a whole or long leg (1 and 2) or divided into a smaller leg (1) and fillet of leg (2).

3. Loin of chump chops are the best chops for grilling, roasting or frying. The loin includes the fillet, the most delicate meat of the lamb. A pair of loins left joined by the backbone gives a handsome joint know as a saddle, which is usually roasted.

4. Best end of neck can be roasted (very impressive when a pair of racks are joined together to make a crown or a guard of honour), grilled or fried.

5. Middle neck chops are excellent braised, but not tender enough for grilling or roasting.

6. Shoulder, a joint some people prefer to the leg as the meat is sweeter and juicier. Makes an excellent roast, either left as it is or boned and stuffed.

7. Scrag-end of neck, an inexpensive cut with a rich flavour. Scrag needs slow, moist cooking to make it tender, an excellent choice for stews and casseroles.

8. Breast. Very fatty and usually braised in stews and casseroles, but when left whole, boned and stuffed, it makes an economical and tasty roast.

pork

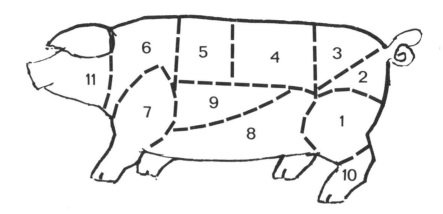

1. and 2. leg	jambon	hesp
3. chump end of leg	pointe de filet	punt van de filet
4. middle loin	côtes au filet	filetkoteletten
5. foreloin	côtes premières	ribstuk 1° rib
6. neck end	côtes spiering	spiering
7. hand (shoulder)	jambon d'épaule	schouder
8. belly	lard maigre	rugbanden
9. spare ribs	spare ribs	spare ribs
10. trotters	pied	poten
11. head	tête	kop

1. et 2. Leg of pork can be roasted or braised whole. A whole leg is too large for most households and the cut is often divided into two parts — (1) knuckle end, (2) fillet end — or sometimes into even smaller joints for roasting.

3. This tender cut is either roasted whole or divided into chops.

4. This cut can be either roasted on the bone or boned and rolled.

5. The foreloin, if left whole for roasting, is called « le carré ». When divided the chops are very tender and sweet and can be grilled or fried.

6. The neck end is a meaty cut interlarded with fatty tissues, which makes it an excellent choice for casseroles. When boned and rolled it makes an economical choice for roasting or braising.

7. The hand or spring (the shoulder), when boned, rolled and trussed, makes a good roasting joint, but long, slow cooking is needed for this coarse-grained cut. When diced it makes a very good stew.

8. Belly pork is usually cured for streaky bacon but can be used fresh for soup and casserole dishes.

9. Spare ribs, grilled or roasted and glazed with a sauce, are a favourite with most families.

10. Trotters need lengthy cooking. The gelatin they contain makes them useful for enriching stews, soups and jellied stocks.

11. Head, very rarely seen in butchers' windows these days but still available on request, is the basis of brawn : « tête pressée ».

index